LEARNING

to

STAY

LEARNING

to

STAY

How God Transformed
My Pain into His Purpose

MICHELLE O'NEIL

ILLUMIFY
MEDIA.COM

The views and opinions expressed in this book are those of the author and do not necessarily reflect the official policy or position of Illumify Media Global.

Published by
Illumify Media Global
www.IllumifyMedia.com
"Let's bring your book to life!"

Some names have been changed to protect people's identities.

Library of Congress Control Number: 2025915433
Paperback ISBN: 979-8-9885629-3-1

Typeset by Art Innovations (http://artinnovations.in/)
Cover design by Debbie Lewis

Printed in the United States of America

Dedicated to my parents and siblings, whose unwavering love and support carried me through the darkest years. And to the friends I've lost to eating disorders and mental illness—and to their families who grieve alongside us. May our stories bring light and hope to those in need.

CONTENTS

PROLOGUE

The ship pitched and rolled beneath an angry sky. Waves crashed against the wooden hull as dark clouds gathered overhead. The helm passed through many hands that night, each sailor certain they could guide the vessel to safety, yet each seafarer steered them further into treacherous waters.

One sailor, his eyes wide with terror, gripped the wheel with white-knuckled hands. Every shadow in the waves became a sea monster, every distant sound a harbinger of doom. He jerked the wheel left and right, overcorrecting with each imagined threat until the ship strayed far from its intended course.

Another sailor shoved him aside, seizing control with an authoritative grip. "We're too heavy!" he shouted above the wind. "We must lighten the ship!" Despite protests from the crew about the precious cargo, he commanded them to throw everything overboard. "It's the only way to survive!" he insisted. As the last crate splashed into the darkness, the ship became a leaf in the wind, too light to cut through the waves, tossed along the surface like a child's toy.

In desperation, a third sailor took the helm, but his shoulders soon slumped in defeat. "What's the use?" he muttered, staring into the impenetrable darkness ahead. "We're doomed. Perhaps we should end it quickly. That iceberg ahead would make quick work of our suffering."

It was then that the old sailor appeared. His weathered face and steady gaze commanded their attention. Without a word, he approached the wheel. The others parted to let him through. From within his rain-soaked coat, he produced a magnificent compass, its brass housing gleaming even in the dim light. Setting it before him, he took the wheel with sure hands, and slowly, steadily began to turn the ship.

The crew watched in amazement as the storm gradually subsided. The clouds parted, revealing hidden stars. As dawn broke across calm waters, a cry rang out from the crow's nest: "Land ho!"

The sailors rushed to the railings, their faces breaking into smiles as they spotted the distant shore. Their relief was palpable—not just for the sight of land, but for the realization that they had survived a treacherous journey that should have destroyed them.

This is my story: a journey through the turbulent seas of mental health. The anxious sailor, the one obsessed with control, the one lost in despair—they were all parts of me, each trying their best to navigate the storm but ultimately steering further from shore. The wise old sailor represents my core Self—the part of my being with wisdom and confidence despite the turbulence. The compass is my faith in Jesus—my one true north when the chaos of life threatens to usurp all sense of direction. In the chapters that follow, I share how I learned to navigate these waters and finally found my way home.

If you told me when I was in sixth grade that in my twenties, I would save lives and welcome infants into the world as a registered nurse, I might have laughed. Actually, I might have cried. No, I probably would have just stared at you blankly and slightly shaken my head.

If you had told me that in my thirties, I would welcome an eleven-year-old girl into my gracefully decorated therapy office, I might have thrown something breakable at the nearest wall. I never expected to be alive in my thirties, let alone preserving lives as a nurse or a counselor.

That's the funny thing about life. It rarely takes you where you expect. As a preteen suffering from severe malnutrition, depression, and panic attacks, I hated counselors and certainly never intended to become one. In high school I pretended to be fine on the outside. I overachieved in academics to assuage the shame I carried from childhood trauma. I thought counselors were phonies who asked multiple questions in various ways to catch their victims in deceit and cognitive distortions. As an early undergrad student, I planned to end my life, believing someone as broken as myself could not help others.

But while I never fathomed where I would be today, God did. He knew coal under pressure can turn into diamonds. His omnipotent hand preserved the life I had given up on more than once. His strength carried me across finish lines to victories I never believed imaginable. That's the story I want to share in these pages. It's not my story. It's God's story. My prayer is that by sharing my journey navigating stormy seas I can offer a small seed of hope to the person who has given up on life or the possibility of a brighter future.

CHAPTER ONE

EARLY DAYS

J grew up in Midland, Texas, living with my parents and siblings. From an outside perspective, I was an all-American middle-class child with an intact family, secure home, and loving parents. Nothing that should have warranted the list of mental and physical health diagnoses assigned to me. Perhaps you can relate?

Society easily invalidates the pain and trauma of our early days when they tell us we had a blessed childhood. Turns out, trauma comes in various shapes and sizes, and even kids born into "perfect families" experience events that leave Grand Canyon–sized scars. While I have countless happy memories of my childhood, difficult memories stand out as influencing the trajectory of my life. I share them not to conjure pity or paint a dismal life but to provide insight into experiences that molded my present.

MY FIRST MEMORY

The first event I recall from my early years is also the first experience I would later label as trauma. Even now, the memory feels like a faded photograph lightly blurred around the edges, but the central image burned into my consciousness with startling clarity.

It was a scorching West Texas summer day, the kind where heat shimmers like a transparent curtain above the ground. We were at a local park, a sprawling landscape of dusty playground equipment and weathered picnic tables. The gathering was a collection of deaf college students and faculty from the junior college where my father worked in Big Spring, Texas. As was typical of such gatherings, hot dogs—simple, classic, quintessentially American—were the centerpiece of our meal.

After hours of unbridled childhood energy—swinging, running, playing—my siblings and I were coated in a layer of sweat and playground dust. My mother called us to the picnic tables, and my older sister, Alicia, my younger brother Aaron, and I lined up on a bench like little soldiers, paper plates of hot dogs before us. In a moment that fractured my childhood innocence, two-year-old Aaron made a fateful decision. He shoved the entire hot dog into his mouth.

What happened next was a nightmare in real time. Aaron began flailing, his tiny hands clutching at his throat in the universal sign of choking terror. The world seemed to simultaneously speed up and slow down. My parents snatched him up, their movements desperate and frantic. Nearby adults quickly whisked Alicia and me to the pavilion's edge, protecting us from what might unfold.

I watched, frozen in complete fear and helplessness, as my parents turned Aaron upside down. They hit his back repeatedly, each strike punctuating their desperation. His skin began to turn an alarming shade of blue, a color that would be forever associated with my first true understanding of mortality.

Sirens pierced the summer air. Two paramedics burst from an ambulance. They grabbed my brother and rushed him into the ambulance's sterile interior. My parents would later tell me they had successfully dislodged the hot dog just before the paramedics arrived, but in that moment, all I understood was raw, unfiltered terror.

That day marked a profound psychological shift. The omnipotent parents I had once imagined—those who could protect me from anything—suddenly seemed devastatingly human. At just four years old, I suddenly understood that life is unpredictable, that safety is an illusion, and that death can intrude without warning.

No longer could I nestle in the comfortable cocoon of childhood innocence. In one breathless moment, I learned that not even the strongest love could guarantee protection from life's uncertainties. Death and danger were not abstract concepts, but real possibilities that could touch anyone at any time.

ADRIENNE, THE SISTER I NEVER KNEW

Another memory from early childhood has etched itself into the landscape of my life like a hidden scar, barely visible but profoundly present.

I already had an older sister and younger brother. Now I was looking forward to having a younger sister. Sadly, while my mother was still pregnant, she began receiving concerning news at her prenatal appointments informing her that the baby in her womb had a generally fatal chromosomal abnormality called trisomy 13. Now, I don't remember a whole lot about what was explained to me or what I understood about my mom's pregnancy complications and diagnosis, but I do remember that there was a feeling of heaviness in the house and talk of praying for a miracle and preparing ourselves in case the baby did not make it. What does "not make it" mean anyway? At age four, I think I just cared that mom was on bedrest and often seemed sad. And being sensitive and empathetic I felt confused, sad, and worried about the future.

When it came time for mom and dad to go to the hospital, my Aunt Yvonna and Uncle Bob came from Colorado to stay with us older three kids at the house. Visits with aunts, uncles, and grandparents were usually exciting occasions, but this time something felt wrong. I have a vivid picture in my mind from this time period of the movie *Willy Wonka* and watching the candy wallpaper scroll down the screen as the credits ran. In fact, I cannot watch *Willy Wonka*, especially the credits, without a pang of grief at losing my sister, Adrienne, before I even had a chance to meet her.

As the credits rolled, the phone rang, and Aunt Yvonna answered. It was clear that the news was not joyous. When she got off the phone, there were tears in her eyes as she stopped the movie and gathered us kids and told us, "Mama had baby Adrienne. She was beautiful, but she did not get to live very long. She got to go meet Jesus soon after she was born. Your mom and dad are fine. They'll be home tomorrow."

What? That was it? No visit to the hospital to see her? No talking on the phone with Mom and Dad? Mom and Dad did, indeed, come home but with nothing but a single 4x6 photo of a lifeless baby with a red rose across her chest to show for their time away. I think I was a little mad. Maybe a lot mad, but mad was not an acceptable feeling in my house at that time in my life— or so I thought. So I just buried it away somewhere along with the tears I did not cry and the questions I did not ask.

My parents really never said much about Adrienne except to explain that God knew what was best and He knew she probably would have had a really painful or hard life, so in His mercy He spared her of that and went ahead and took her home early so she wouldn't have to suffer any of the things in this world. Hmm, interesting explanation for a preschooler to grasp.

As I grew up, I repeated this explanation to myself over and over. When asked how many kids were in my family, I told my teachers and therapists, "There are three of us here and one in heaven." I never gave this answer if my parents were standing by because this topic of conversation seemed to be taboo. They never talked about it or listed her when naming their children to curious acquaintances. But to me, she is my sister whether I met her or not, and she is a part of my family. Some part of me longed to be able to process and talk about this and receive comfort and empathy, even if from a stranger at church or the grocery store.

I always knew when it was Adrienne's birthday because mom would become emotional for a few days and spend more time in her room and come out with a red face saying everything was fine and, "I just needed a nap." Around five to six years of age, I would sneak to the big oak china cabinet in the living room, climb on a stool, and after making sure no one was looking, open the glass doors behind which sat the china baby booties with each of my sibling's names and birthdates painted on them. This was the only thing in the whole house that proved I had a younger sister and put her name and birthdate in writing for all to see. I would stand on my tiptoes on that stool and run my fingers over the cold, smooth china bootie and fondle the pink satin ribbon shoelaces on the top.

My thoughts and emotions swirled, and I felt disconnected from present reality.

I wondered what my mom would think if she caught me. My actions felt so rebellious and sneaky. But I just want to feel close to my younger sister. I didn't understand why no one else in the house seemed to have questions and feelings. I always figured I was just the odd one. Stuff that bothered no one else bothered me. I wished I could just turn off that part of my brain.

Back then, the loss seemed to float at the edges of my family's consciousness, a delicate almost invisible thread woven into our family tapestry. My parents and early therapists seemed to brush it aside as insignificant. But memories aren't always loud; sometimes they are the quietest wounds, the most subtle imprints that shape who we become. Adrienne was more than a name, more than a brief moment of potential. She was an unwritten chapter, a sister who existed in the tender space between what was and what could have been.

HOMESCHOOLING ADVENTURES

For many people, the term "homeschooler" might bring certain assumptions to mind. Perhaps a large family dressed in hand-sewn gingham meticulously practicing cursive on weathered newspaper scraps around a massive oak farmhouse table. Let me shatter that narrow stereotype with the vibrant reality of my own experience.

Contrary to popular misconceptions, homeschooling families are not monolithic. Children are not confined to isolated bubbles, interacting only with those within our own four walls. The diversity of homeschooling experiences is as wide and varied as the families who choose this educational path. Students don't all wear pilgrim costumes or perpetual pajamas, and our education is far more structured and comprehensive than most realize.

In my own experience, the curriculum wasn't a choose-your-own-adventure of endless fascinating topics conveniently sidestepping state standards. We were accountable, challenged, and rigorously prepared. The myth that homeschoolers drift through education, learning only what captures their fleeting interest, couldn't be further from the truth.

And perhaps most importantly, we were not destined to become social outcasts—awkward time travelers unable to navigate the complexities of modern society. The stereotype of the homeschooled child as a socially inept monk accidentally wandering into a bustling casino is not just inaccurate, it's insulting. We were learning, growing, and preparing to engage with the world in meaningful, nuanced ways.

My homeschooling experience was a rich, dynamic journey of intellectual and personal growth far from the simplistic caricatures often presented in popular imagination.

During my freshman year at college, when I told people that I was homeschooled from second to ninth grade, I heard statements such as, "What? You seem so normal! You know how to talk to people." Perhaps I don't know exactly what everyone else envisions when they think of homeschoolers, but I tend to consider the fact that I was homeschooled for most of my elementary and junior high years one of the least impactful facets of my childhood.

Now, don't get me wrong; being homeschooled is not a benign element of my past. My siblings may feel differently about homeschooling than I do. Personally, I believe it helped me excel academically, thrive creatively, and build a solid Christian foundation of faith. My mother worked as a geological engineer and my father earned a master's in microbiology. When I say homeschooling helped me excel academically, I credit my professor and principal (mom and dad respectively), who ensured my siblings and I were well versed in all subjects. By this point I had two younger brothers as well as my older sister, making our school enrollment a grand total of four. (My adopted brother did not enter the picture until I was in high school, and with our age gap I did not get to enjoy homeschooling adventures with him.)

Our daily schedule looked like this: Wake up at 7 a.m. Dress and arrive at the breakfast table by 7:30 a.m. Finish chores and prepare for lessons by 8:15 a.m. We began the day with a pledge of allegiance to the American flag followed by a rousing rendition of some upbeat patriotic song as the chosen sibling waved the flag and led the rest running around the house singing loudly.

With our blood pumping and the flag back in the pencil holder made from a family-sized baked beans can lovingly decorated with colorful construction paper, my mother began individual lessons, starting with the eldest sibling. We referred to a lesson plan hanging on the wall for direction in what needed to be accomplished that day. When it was not our turn for lessons with mom, we worked on the assigned pages of a grammar workbook, read our science text, worked on math homework, or practiced reciting our memory work, such as a poem by Longfellow or the Gettysburg Address.

History and science ranked as my favorite subjects. Once I transitioned to public high school, history became one of my least favorite subjects, probably because it felt lifeless compared to my mother's teaching method. Each semester we studied a different time period. Mom read aloud both nonfiction and fiction books about the era. We sometimes wrote essays or researched related topics, fairly normal assignments, I suppose.

We also worked on creative projects, such as making salt dough maps painted with watercolor, sewing costumes to match the traditional clothing of the time, and inviting our friends or grandparents to a feast and theatrical performance at the end of a semester. How many of you can say that you know how ancient Egyptian women did their makeup because you and your sister practiced using charcoal to paint elongated eyebrows on each other before donning your freshly sewn white Egyptian *kalasiris* tunics?

Science was my first true love, a passion ignited by the access to my biology professor dad's full-service science lab. Some of my most cherished childhood memories are steeped in scientific exploration, each experiment a doorway to wonder and discovery.

I still recall the excitement of boiling agar and carefully pouring our own petri dishes, then meticulously streaking them with samples collected from around our house. We watched with breathless anticipation as colorful molds, cocci, and bacilli blossomed in the incubator, each plate creating a miniature universe of microbial life waiting for understanding.

Our scientific adventures knew no bounds. Take, for instance, the day we persuaded the local butcher to save a bovine eyeball from the cow my family raised. A dissection lab followed in our garage, spread across a ping pong table covered in trash bags. Our homeschooling co-op gathered, a mix of wide-eyed excitement with barely contained queasiness, as we explored the intricate anatomy of an eye.

My scientific curiosity deepened with age. In high school biology, during a cat dissection lab, I somehow convinced my teacher to let me continue my research at home. My mother, typically patient with my scientific pursuits, reluctantly agreed to host the specimen "for one afternoon only" before a proper burial. Her measured tolerance spoke volumes about her understanding of my passionate learning style.

Looking back, I realize I was fortunate. My educational experience—a rich, vibrant journey of scientific exploration that stretched far beyond traditional classroom boundaries—was anything but ordinary. This solid academic foundation would prove crucial, providing me a stable intellectual anchor during the internal storms of later years. As you'll discover, this early love of science enabled me to remain at the top of my class in high school and college, even as personal challenges churned beneath the surface.

My early years showed me that childhood is not just one thing. It is a mixed bag. The same kitchen table where we spread our schoolbooks for homeschool lessons was the same table where we also gathered to comfort one another in our times of grief. What I did not have words for then, but was learning day by day, is that those who love you can't shield you from all harm, but they will be there to hold you when life feels like it is falling apart. Looking back, the memories—the silly ones and the scary ones—are all part of the same story. A story that paved the way to the person I am today.

CHAPTER TWO

LONELY AND CONFUSED

"*D*id you see how Emily was talking to Brady before the lesson started? I think she has a major crush on him."

"Yeah, and she keeps wearing those tank tops and new little skirts her mom lets her buy from Forever 21. I totally think she likes him."

Sixth-grade Sunday school class at the large Southern Baptist church I faithfully attended all my growing up years was a time for girls to wear their newest outfits and fantasize about their latest crush. All the while, the boys just stood in huddles talking about sports and eating as many chocolate-glazed donuts as they could before the teacher broke up the gossip circles to start that weeks' Bible lesson.

I suppose this was normal pre-teen behavior. But what did I know? I was not normal. At least, that is how I felt and what I told myself. Maybe I just did not really care about boys and clothes and going to the mall. Or perhaps I did not want to admit to my peers or even to myself that my parents were not in favor of boyfriends at this age and had rules against wearing tank tops and skirts that landed much above the knee. Looking back, I think it was a combination of the two, but either way I just did not fit in. I was not normal and that left me feeling lonely, confused, and angry.

The problem is that lonely, confused, and angry are not safe or acceptable emotions in most people's eyes. This was the constant swirling of thoughts inside my eleven-year-old brain:

You cannot express your feelings of discomfort, disappointment, or sadness. Remember, Mom says there is always someone who has it worse than you do, so be grateful and keep a positive attitude. Complaining and grumbling won't get you anywhere. Don't judge others. If the problem can't be them, it must be me. I am the problem. I must be sinning. I need to do better. Try harder. Pray more. Talk less. But I thought the Bible said to love God more than clothes and to prioritize helping others and obeying your parents over spending hours talking about how cute a boy is or what

*new outfit I want to buy to impress everyone at school. Why,
then, am I the wrong one and my friends at church the
ones in the right? I must be the problem. I have to take the
responsibility for whatever feels bad or wrong in my life.*

It is common for all preteens go through a period of
feeling left out and struggling with friends and identity.
There are many different ways in which preteens react
and cope with feelings and changes. While I had a loving
and supportive family, somehow I believed that negative
feelings were bad and should not be expressed. I grappled
with my thoughts and feelings constantly.

The mindset started to eat me alive, figuratively as well
as literally. Since I was homeschooled, a lot of my social
interaction took place at church. These church "friends" I
had grown up with no longer felt like friends and seemed
to have forgotten that I existed. I still attended Sunday
school, children's choir, Bible Drill, Girl's in Action, and
Upward Sports basketball league with these peers, but I
started to shut down, to close off, to stop interacting and
laughing with the other girls.

Somewhere between fifth and sixth grade I started to
lose connection with my peers as well as myself. Perhaps I
never felt fully connected. I remember enjoying talking to
my friends' parents more than my friends on homeschool
co-op park days. I would try to force myself to connect

in some way with the other kids my age, but that only left me feeling more confused as to who I truly was in the first place.

There were many things that bothered me that I kept inside, not even telling my parents. Perhaps I did not even fully acknowledge them to myself. Certain behaviors and obsessive and compulsive thoughts can feel so much like a part of oneself that one doesn't question them even when one knows that such behavior is not normal. For me this looked like needing to touch things an even number of times or compulsively manipulating my steps so that I stepped over sidewalk cracks the same number of times with the right foot as with the left. Lying in bed at night, I would sometimes get distracted by the sensation of my toes touching one another unequally and have to spend time adjusting my position and the weight of the blankets on top of me to alleviate the discomfort. If I accidentally touched myself with my fingernail, I immediately needed to smooth over the skin I touched with the pad of my finger. Compulsively I would rub the skin where my nail touched three times, followed by rubbing my nail the same number of times. Three times was the magic number. Numbers had personalities in my head. The number two was bratty. Four was a snob. One was just not enough. Three was a quiet number that felt complete and peaceful. Until this process of carefully numbered rubbing was complete, I could not focus on anything else. Sufice it to say, I felt like my thoughts and compulsions set me apart from all of my peers and that if they knew them, they would never speak to me again.

Then there were my siblings. I often felt like I was so different from them as well. My older sister liked to sleep in and read books. I woke up early and preferred playing with Hot Wheels cars outside in the dirt, making stick shelters for my stuffed bunny, or pretending to be Laura Ingalls Wilder. My brothers often squabbled (like typical brothers), and the noise and conflict caused so much tension and discomfort inside I would try to make them stop. I realize now I had some sensory sensitivities and OCD symptoms, but at the time I did not know how to verbalize my discomfort or anxiety and just told myself I was the problem. I went outside or got lost in my imagination to avoid it. Though I enjoyed playing together with my siblings and friends, I never felt I quite fit in with them, or even myself.

Something has to change, I thought. *What is it that they don't like about me? Is it just because I don't talk about boys or wear the same trendy clothes? Or is it because I talk too much? I do tend to be one of the first to answer the questions or volunteer to participate in class. I thought those were good things. But maybe they just see me as an annoying Goody Two-shoes, a teacher's pet, a Bible nerd. Maybe if I change myself, stop talking and answering questions, be the shy girl in the corner instead of the loud one on the front row, I will find a place and fit in.*

As I gave in to this belief and began to withdraw in social settings and tell myself to not talk unless absolutely necessary, I started to shrink and shrivel inside and out. A heavy, dark depression set in. The eleven-year-old girl who was usually making up silly games, creating art from leaves and horsehair found in the back pasture, and daydreaming about being a world-class surgeon started to spend her free time alone in the back pasture or garden crying where no one would see her tears. I still did not feel safe crying in front of others, especially my parents, so I tried to hide my negative feelings. As is common, the depression quickly led to a lack of appetite, which led to a habit of restriction, which led to brain changes that caused extreme anxiety about food and eating.

At the time, if you asked me why I would not eat, I would have said, "I am just too scared."

"Scared of what?" my parents would ask.

"I don't know," I would reply with a downcast face, eyes full of fear and shame. First my shoulders would shake and then my whole body as I sobbed and hyperventilated. This ensued shortly after someone asked me about my fear of food. I could not tell you why I feared food, I just knew that it was an uncontrollable fear. I felt gross if I ate and guilty for eating anything that tasted relatively pleasant.

Somewhere inside I believed that I did not deserve pleasure and since for most people eating is a pleasureful experience, it became a source of fear, guilt, shame, and confusion for me. Yet, at the same time, when my parents would tell me to eat—beg me to eat—I would feel horribly guilty and shameful for being a disobedient daughter as well. I faced a constant war inside. I could please my parents and feel disgusting and guilty for eating. Or I could follow the strict unwritten rules inside my head about what foods were good and allowed and which ones were bad or off limits.

When I told my parents that I felt guilty for eating and would not take bites myself, they sometimes took me to the back bedroom and spoon-fed me themselves. They would tell me, "you can't feel guilty for eating if you're not the one doing it." While I know they were just scared and desperate, these times of being more or less force fed in the back room only further reinforced the message that I was broken and needed to be separated from my siblings. Eating became a traumatic experience for me.

Those who have experienced eating disorders, specifically anorexia nervosa, can relate to the internal tug-of-war. And the obsessive thoughts and compulsive behaviors are only intensified. Counting, sorting, and obsessing over food and calories consumed my mind to the point that I asked my mom if it was possible to get a brain transplant or wipe my memory and start over. Recent statistics show that recent statistics show that about 28 million Americans suffer from a diagnosable eating disorder and 10,200 deaths each year are related to an eating disorder.[1] Many of these deaths are suicide-related due to the severity of inner turmoil sufferers of eating disorders experience along with comorbidities of anxiety and depression.

My parents took me to doctors, psychiatrists, and counselors in an attempt to "fix" the problem that was me. My level of compliance resembled a prison camp inmate who has lost his will to escape or fight back. I was unenthused at the constant visits to cold, sterile offices with stern, unsmiling adults in long white lab coats who sat behind oversized mahogany desks and said things I did not understand but made my mother blink back tears.

My dad tried to play into my smart, logical side by giving me a big notebook in which I would log my food intake. He found one of Mom's cookbooks from the 1980s that had a calorie count appendix in the back. He taught me to look up the foods I ate and write the food along with the calorie content in my notebook, encouraging me to reach a daily total that felt unattainable and terrifying.

While I learned a lot from this, it did not produce the result my parents hoped for. Instead, my already malnourished, irrational thought patterns only worsened as I learned to equate numbers with the foods I already feared. I ended up performing constant calculations in my head and took a headlong dive into the deep-sea territory of obsessive-compulsive disorder—a common comorbidity of eating disorders and anxiety.

It did not take long for me to reach a state of physical as well as mental decline that forced my parents into making some big decisions. "She needs a higher level of care," the psychiatrist told my parents in a grim follow-up meeting. "She is not responding satisfactorily to the medications yet, and we do not have time to wait on a medication change that may or may not prove effective. Your daughter's life is in the balance. Frankly, I'd be surprised if she ever fully recovers, but at least you can hope to give her some more time by sending her to an inpatient treatment center. You can expect this to be her life from now on. I rarely see cases like this fully recovering or finding their way to a prosperous adulthood."

With my suitcase packed, I found myself boarding an airplane and crossing the threshold of one of the only residential level treatment centers for eating and mental health disorders that would accept an eleven-year-old. What lay ahead would change my life forever.

CHAPTER THREE

WITHOUT CONSENT

*T*he thing about being a minor is you feel like you don't have any decision-making power. You are forced to go to school and forced to go to bed at a certain time. Most children's daily schedules, meals, and decisions about whether or not to get a yearly flu shot are made by their guardians. Had you asked me at age nine or ten if I had choices, I would have said, "Yes, of course." But then if you asked me if it was my choice to do daily lessons from my *Shurley Grammar* workbook, I would have said, "No, Mom makes me do that."

To be honest, I do not know where the line is between parents making decisions for their children and children making decisions for themselves. I wish there was a big black line with flashing lights that is obvious and easy to follow. Unfortunately, it is more of a gray line with blurred edges. I do not blame my parents for causing physical or emotional trauma. I blame sin—which fuels all of the evil acts of mankind on this broken planet until Jesus returns to set this world of violence, abuse, and illness straight once and for all.

The reason I share my story is not to cast blame or shame anyone, healthcare professionals or even myself. I understand the tension and weight of matters such as liability, risk, and tough love. If I had an anti-treatment approach, I would not have chosen nursing or counseling professions. Instead, I share about the trauma I incurred through involuntary medical treatments and procedures in order to shed light on a gray topic that is often ignored but needs to be addressed for the sake of our vulnerable children and youth (and adults for that matter).

So there I was, age eleven, at a residential treatment center for eating and mental health disorders. I was confused, angry, hurt, and afraid after waving goodbye to my parents. A nurse ushered me into a cold, sterile office. She gave a smile that was meant to put me at ease but did little to calm the butterflies in my empty stomach.

"You have to take everything off," she said. "Including your undergarments. You can put on this paper gown, which is what we will use for daily morning weigh-ins and vitals." I stared at her blankly, unable to register what she was telling me or translate it into actionable steps. "Well, you can go ahead and start undressing now. I have to stay here and watch to make sure you aren't hiding any sharp objects and document any scars or tattoos you have. It's standard procedure; I'm sure this isn't your first time sitting for a strip search." The nurse riffled through some papers in a pale-yellow file with my name on the front as she watched me with an all-seeing side-eye.

Scars? Tattoos? Not my first time? What is she talking about? I wondered. *Of course I have never been strip-searched. I don't even know what that means, but if this is what it is, I'll be sure to avoid it at all costs for the rest of my life. Mom and Dad always said we should not show our special parts except to our mom or our future husband or to let the pediatrician check us once a year to make sure we are healthy everywhere. Surely, they would not have brought me here if they knew I was going to have to undress in front of a stranger!*

My mind spun with a thousand thoughts, but somehow my arms and legs moved on their own. Soon I was standing stark naked in front of a nurse whose name I did not even know. I hurriedly put on the paper gown and tried to wrap it around my bony frame for both warmth and safety. The thin paper did little to shield from either the cold or the probing eyes.

Normally, when working with a client who has extreme fears, a therapist would first teach some basic coping skills, build rapport, and ensure a sense of safety in the client before jumping into any forms of exposure therapy. Not so here. Day one proceeded as follows: Survive the strip search, visit the vampire for your first of fifty blood draws, then take a seat at a table of strangers and stare your fear straight in the face.

At the dinner table, they exposed me to every food that I was afraid of. It was as though they wanted to build as much anxiety in me as they could. And to add to it, there was a list of table rules that were meant to keep patients from engaging in eating disorder behaviors. They called it redirection, which is a nice way of saying they constantly criticized us at the table for such things as eating too fast, eating too slow, cutting your food up too small, taking too small of bites, putting your hands in your lap, wiping grease off your lips with a napkin, talking about food, talking about fears, talking about calories, not talking, staring at your plate too long, staring across the room, not engaging with your peers at the table, and the list goes on. Afterward, the table monitor would push her hands into your pockets to ensure that everything on the plate made it to your mouth.

While I can understand and appreciate the reason for these rules, I also know firsthand how much anxiety it produces in a young perfectionist girl who is terrified of the world and especially of those in a position of authority over her. If I had not already been disconnected from mealtimes and unable to eat with any amount of mindfulness, I am sure this atmosphere would have quickly brought on the state of detachment from meals.

And so, I tearfully picked at the dry, bland chicken breast, rice pilaf, and butter-soaked green beans on my plate while being instructed to stop cutting my green beans in half and to eat my rice with a spoon instead of a fork. Caring not what the food tasted like, my brain was somewhere else as I mechanically put pieces of food in my mouth without acknowledging any flavor, texture, smell, or temperature.

It is not uncommon among eating disorder sufferers to dissociate from food as a protective mechanism. Feelings of shame and unworthiness prevent you from enjoying the taste of food, and sufferers even fear that if food tastes good it must be bad for you.

I barely got through half of my chicken breast and a quarter of the beans before time was called, and the table monitor said we must get up from the table and have our pockets checked. One other girl and I still had food on our plates. With a dissatisfied humph, the table monitor announced, "the two of you need to go to the nurse's station now for boosting."

Boosting? What could that mean? I imagined it was not a good thing.

I followed the girl with the tangled black hair to the nurse's station where we took seats on the chairs that lined the wall. Rules were posted on the door and wall outside the nurse's office: TAKE A SEAT WHILE WAITING FOR MEDS and PLEASE MAKE SURE TO STICK YOUR TONGUE OUT FOR THE NURSE FOR PILL CHECK AFTER SWALLOWING PILLS and LAB DRAWS ARE MONDAY AND WEDNESDAY 5:30-6:30 A.M.: DON'T BE LATE!

Do I really have to get blood drawn twice a week? What is a pill check? And why are there signs everywhere telling us to sit down?

It did not take long to find out the answer to all of my questions. Inside the nurse's office—really more of a closet with a cabinet full of lab supplies, pill bottles, and first aid supplies—I waited on another chair while the nurse measured out some thick white liquid and told me about the various rules and protocols of the treatment center.

"Boosting" was the term given to receiving supplementation of the Boost brand meal replacement shake that they gave us to make up for any food not eaten at a meal or snack. We could choose between strawberry, chocolate, or vanilla. If we refused boosting we would have privileges removed, such as no yoga, no outing on the weekend, or no equine therapy. Those on the first day didn't even have any of those privileges yet, so the privilege of walking to groups, meals, or the bedroom would be taken away, and we'd be assigned to couch rest. I was warned that I did not want to know what would happen if someone continued to refuse the supplementation, and that disobeying couch rest resulted in one-on-one monitoring. I felt absolutely nauseous as I tried to drink the thick, tepid liquid. My mind raced, trying to calculate how many calories were in the food I ate and if what I had left on my plate was equivalent to the amount of liquid in my cup.

I think they over filled my cup. This has to be too much. My stomach can't handle this. I think I think I'm going to be sick.

Apparently, being sick was also not an option. When I said I felt nauseous and asked for the bathroom, the girl with the messy black hair sitting next to me with strawberry liquid in her glass laughed and almost choked.

The nurse glared at me over her clipboard. "Using the restroom is prohibited for one hour after each meal and thirty minutes after each snack. If you refuse to finish your supplementation, I'll make a status change to couch rest for you and perhaps you should try the vanilla flavor next time."

Is she serious? I thought. *I only chose strawberry because the other girl did, so I assumed it was the safer choice. Can't use the bathroom? What sort of prison is this? What if I pee my pants or vomit on the carpet? This can't be real. I have to wake up from this nightmare!*

I have no idea how, but I finally swallowed the last mouthful of cotton-candy-pink liquid. The nurse sighed, "There. Next time I won't let you take so long. Boosting period is no more than five minutes after a meal, and I just allowed you ten. You'll be late to group processing."

The other girl had already finished and left. I stared at the nurse, wondering where the group room was. I imagined my mouth moving to ask her but realized that no sound was coming out.

"Oh, you don't know where to go do you?" the nurse asked. "Fine. I'll show you, but I have to lock the nurse's station to walk you there." Another impatient sigh. I waited as she locked the door and put a key ring with at least a dozen keys on it into her scrub pocket. Then she motioned for me to follow her.

"Uh, yeah, thanks." I mumbled as I followed her down the hallway.

It is still hard for me to fully remember or even try to think through what happened in the next few days at the treatment center. While I was told that this was saving my life, I felt like it was removing all life as I knew it and replacing it with a twilight-zone-like chamber of horrors. My daily routine became waking up at 5:00 a.m. to have a night monitor watch me pee in a bathroom stall, wearing a paper gown to the nurse's station for vitals and weights, and then facing three meals and three snacks, alternating with group therapy sessions and meetings with psychiatrists and dietitians.

Because I was somewhat in shock, I did not talk very much at first. Instead, I spent a lot of time observing the other patients. At eleven I was the youngest resident because the treatment center usually only took people aged twelve to seventeen, but an exception had been made for me due to my severe condition and need for immediate care. There were only females, at least in my building, but the ages, histories, and mental health diagnoses varied.

I remember one seventeen-year-old girl named Brigette who had arms full of tattoos and pink tinged hair used to sit cross-legged on the floor and stare off into space. Eventually the nurses would come and pull her off the floor and lead her to the nurse's station where she would stay until she was feeling better. When I finally got the nerve to ask what was wrong, she told me more than I wanted to know. She had been sexually abused all through her childhood and indifferently proclaimed with a hint of pride, "So now I have flashbacks and dissociate and sometimes have catatonic seizures because of it. This place is supposed to help, but that's a joke. This is my third time to go to one of these places, and it never gets better. The only thing that works is getting high, but I got caught too many times so now I just refuse to eat and get my own high that way."

I stared at her in disbelief.

"You're lucky," she continued. "Looks like you've never been through any trauma like me. Maybe you can actually recover—whatever that means."

While I did not connect with many of the other patients or even my therapist, I did connect immediately with the horses. Equine therapy soon became my favorite part of the week. The long trail rides through hills covered with saguaro cactus were my solace. I had always enjoyed nature, but now more than ever the connection to the horse beneath me and the grounding landscape around me brought a sense of calm that I needed now more than ever.

There was another girl, closer to my age, who had a long plastic tube coming out of one nostril and taped to her cheek. I noticed a few others who had this device, and it did not take long to learn what it was. I had never seen a nasogastric tube before. They used it for nighttime feeding, which would soon become all too familiar.

"Does it hurt?" I asked my roommate Frances on the second night after the nurse pushed water into her tube through a syringe and listened to her stomach with a stethoscope.

"No, but I hate the cold-water flush. It's better when they warm the water first. As long as the formula is room temperature, you don't really feel anything. It's better than having to eat three thousand calories all in meals," Frances said nonchalantly.

"No calorie talk, remember," the nurse interrupted as she hooked the end of the tube that was taped to Frances' cheek to another long tube connected to a pump and a large bag of thick liquid.

"Right, sorry. I just mean the tube isn't so bad once you get used to it. You'll probably get one soon." Frances neatly arranged all of her stuffed animals around her in her bed as the nurse programmed the pump to run the formula through her tube slowly throughout the night.

"No way," I said. "I finished all of my meals today. I'm not getting one of those." I stared at Frances and the pump for a few more seconds until the nurse walked to the door, switched off the light, and called to the night room monitor to take her place on the chair by the doorway where she would watch us sleep. Apparently, if no one was watching, some girls would try to do crunches or leg lifts in their beds or even unhook their feeding tubes. I couldn't imagine breaking any rules in this place because it seemed like a prison camp, but I guess not everyone was a class A rule follower like me.

On day three, everything still felt surreal, but I forced myself to complete the meals and snacks placed before me so I would not have to endure boosting again. I thought everything was going well until I met with the dietitian for my weekly one-on-one session.

"Well, Michelle," she said. "It looks like you have been completing more of your meals and snacks than on day one, but you are still on the lowest meal plan. And your weight is not stabilizing. Sometimes this happens when you have a fast metabolism. The body quickly utilizes all the nutrition you take in and then you need even more in order to gain weight. Given your condition of severe malnutrition and frighteningly low BMI, we are going to have to place a nasogastric tube for nighttime feedings in order to meet the caloric requirements your body will need to gain weight and repair the damage you have done to your internal organs." The dietitian did not even make eye contact with me as she continued. "Tube feeding is the gold standard of treatment for cases of anorexia nervosa like yours," she said. "It will be so much more comfortable for you this way."

"No," I blurted out.

"Excuse me?"

"No. I don't want a tube in my nose. I'll just eat more if I have to, but I do not want the tube." I shuddered when I said the word and imagined the long piece of spaghetti-like plastic taped to my cheek and snaking its way down my nose and throat.

"I'm sorry, Michelle. I understand that you do not want it, but it is not up to you. I already called and talked to your parents before we met, and they signed consent to have the tube placed today. You are a minor, so consent comes from your parents not you. They know how to make the best decisions for your health, and the doctors here told them all the best practices and recommendations."

"My mom told you to do this? I don't believe you. I don't want it. You can't make me!" I started to tear up, and it felt like my throat was full of flaming hair balls.

"It's always hard on you young ones. That's why we don't like to take on cases like yours. Anyway, you'll get used to it, Michelle. You can talk to your mom about it when you get phone time this week. Don't forget to sign up on the nurse's station door for you twice a week fifteen-minute phone slots. They fill up fast with the high census we have here right now." She closed the file in her lap and stood. "I'll walk you to the nurse's station now. I already told them to get everything ready for your tube. Once it's in, the staff will drive you over to the clinic five minutes away for a quick X-ray to confirm correct placement and then we can start feedings tonight. Easy peasy."

You have to be kidding me. I cannot have some foreign object placed in my body against my will. What did I do wrong? I followed all the rules. I was only reprimanded for standing too long one time, and I sat down immediately. I never hid any food in my pockets, and I take all of my meds as told, even the chalky orange calcium tablet that I almost refused the second day.

"Just let me drink the stuff at night instead," I pleaded with tears in my eyes. The staff would not budge.

"Look here, your parents gave verbal consent for the procedure. It's on this form right here, see. If you cooperate, it won't take long or hurt hardly at all." The nurse shoved a consent form under my nose that explained the risks involved with placing a nasogastric tube. My parents' names were written at the bottom with the words "telephone consent obtained" and today's date beneath it. "Now, you are going to drink this cup of water with this straw, and as you swallow, I will push the tube into your nose. Keep swallowing to help guide it down your throat. It might feel a little scratchy, but it shouldn't really hurt, and it will all be over soon. Then we will tape it down. In a day or two, you will forget it is there. It will feel like it is just another part of your body."

I was already crying, but the tears came more heavily as they began pushing the rubber tube into my nostril and down the back of my throat. I started to gag. My nose burned, and I thought I was going to throw up or pass out or both. "Keep swallowing!" the nurse reminded as she used one hand to shove the tube farther down my throat and the other hand to push the cup of water and straw closer to my mouth. I thought I was going to choke; it felt like my airway was closing off, so I sipped and swallowed the water through the straw in a desperate attempt to bring this torture to an end. Finally, the nurse stopped shoving the tube and told me to stop swallowing. She ripped a piece of tape off of a roll and stuck the tube to my cheek, leaving about five inches of tubing dangling by my neck. "All done!" she exclaimed. "Now, you can go on out and join the milieu for open art time until the driver is ready to take you for the X-ray."

I attended the last group meeting of the day but got little out of it since all I could think about was the fact that I had a foreign object inside me and attached to my face for all to see. It felt like a badge of shame, saying, "Look how bad I've messed up. Since they say I am not competent to take care of my body, they are going to turn me into a machine instead."

It is hard to explain how utterly dehumanizing it felt to have a piece of medical equipment living inside me against my will. The emotional distress only multiplied when it came time to be hooked up that night for my first feeding. I had felt disconnected from my self before, but being force fed in bed at night was going to a much deeper level. Each night, as I lay in the bed, squeezing myself into as tight a ball as possible, I completely disconnected from my physical shell, as if watching myself from above.

As a professional now, I understand that this is a fairly common trauma response. When the brain and body experience something too distressing to tolerate or comprehend, the brain uses a little trick called depersonalization to detach itself from the body and separate the mind from the bodily trauma taking place. This depersonalization is a type of dissociation, which is a broader term for feeling disconnected from one's mind, body, thoughts, or identity.

I experienced depersonalization and dissociation regularly during this time in my life as a way of coping with the feelings of body violation, shame, and fear. The most intense times of dissociation were at night when the nurse came into the room to hook up the feeding tube. She would roll in an IV pole with a clear plastic bag hanging from it and that was connected to a purple piece of machinery that everyone called the Kangaroo pump. First, she would get out her stethoscope and place its cold bell on my abdomen as she shot a syringe full of cold water into the tube. She called this "checking placement." I called it torture.

Little did I know that years later I would be initiating NG tube feedings for infants in the NICU or children with special needs as a practicing registered nurse. Fortunately, I had a good therapist by that time who helped me process the PTSD symptoms that would surface in those later years when the roles were reversed, and I was the nurse standing over the patient in bed. Fortunately, I had the empathy to conduct this skill with a different level of care and compassion than the nurses who treated me.

I can hear the Kangaroo pump priming the tubing and the motor running in my mind to this day. Even before the nurse came in, I would shut my eyes as tight as possible, hold the end of my tube tightly in my fist, and start to leave my body while sobbing and hyperventilating under the covers. Sometimes I would imagine being in a different place. Other times I would just repeat words over and over in my head such as, "Why is this happening?" "God, please make it stop," or "I just want to die. I just want to die." Eventually the nurse would pry the end of the tube out of my fist. She would try to say something lighthearted before becoming irritated at my obstinance and demand that I let go of the tubing. All the while, I would keep my eyes shut and act as if I did not hear her. I wasn't really *there* to hear her anyway. I was watching myself from my seat on a cloud above my bed. Numb to the bodily sensations by this time, I would eventually become detached enough from the trauma and, exhausted from crying, fall asleep. This is an experience I would wish on no one. It built a strong pattern inside me of dissociation as a coping mechanism for numbing unwanted thoughts, feelings, emotions, or experiences that would last into adulthood.

Unfortunately, dissociation ended up robbing me of the ability to connect in some important ways to the present moment. I would have to spend many years working with a trauma-informed therapist to recognize when I start to dissociate and use grounding skills to remain in the present moment instead of detaching from reality. Nevertheless, I am thankful to the dissociative part of me that protected me from feelings that I could not tolerate at that time and even later in life when I would again want to escape from pain. While I cannot say for sure that I would have ended my life if it weren't for this coping skill (maladaptive as it may be), I am positive that I would have engaged in many more self-destructive behaviors in an attempt to assuage the pain if it were not for the escape I learned to quickly fall into by dissociating when things felt too hard to bear.

My experience at a residential treatment center at age eleven was traumatic. I would not have this fact validated or acknowledged until adulthood. And so I spent many years blaming myself for the irrational, involuntary responses I had toward being asked to undress or step on a scale at a doctor's visit, for jumping at sounds in the night, or closing down when threatened by my therapist or dietitian that "if you lose even one more pound you will need to go back to a higher level of care." At age eleven, and until much later, I thought trauma was only something experienced by people who went into military combat or were sexually assaulted. At the time, I was just surviving, going through the motions, attempting to understand what was happening to me, and wondering if life would ever feel normal again.

Later in life I would look back and realize how the experiences in Arizona at age eleven led me to live out the next decade or so of my life in a state of mind-body detachment, constant shame, and never-ending fear of abandonment. Eleven-year-olds who have learned to detach and disassociate should never be placed at the helm of a ship—a guaranteed set up for disaster.

On the bright side, through these experiences I gained insight and empathy that has allowed me to touch the lives of other trauma survivors. It would be easier to say that I wish this had not happened to me. However, believing that my life is not to be lived for me but for God's glory and to help others, I am thankful for the experiences that allow me to connect to and help others at a deeper level than would have been possible had I not endured trauma myself. And I thank God for keeping me alive through the years of struggle and providing others to help in my journey toward healing so that I did not remain a victim to this trauma all my life. The same is possible for you, my friend.

About two-thirds of the way through my stay, my parents were allowed to visit. It was Easter. For a week ahead of time my therapist and dietitian talked to me about the rules of visitation, guidelines for Easter dinner with parents, and reminders to lean on staff for support if big emotions arose.

Finally, the day arrived. "Time to head to the dining hall!" Called the therapist, signaling for all the patients to wrap up their journaling, napping, or whatever leisure time activity they were busying themselves with to walk together to the dining hall across from the Big House, where we slept.

I stepped into the now familiar dining hall and was met with an unfamiliar sight. There was my dad, holding a purple stuffed bunny. Next to him, my mom. Not quite crying, not quite smiling. They looked so out of place. I'm guessing they felt out of place as well. Awkwardly, I walked over to them, and my mom wrapped me in a big hug, followed by my dad. It had been over a month since I last saw them—the day they dropped me off here. It felt like a lifetime ago. As much as I missed them and as glad as I was to see them, my emotions felt all mixed like when water spills on paint and all lines and definition become blurred and indiscernible.

Are they mad? Are they sad? Oh, they must be staring at this tube in my nose, I thought. *Maybe they are regretting giving consent for every little thing my treatment team tells them I need done to me. Now that I've been turned into a chubby little robot with spaghetti hanging out of her nostril, they will decide to disown me for good.*

No—I know that is not true. They still love me. They are just scared and desperate to get me help. Every week on our phone call I can hear in their voices how much they ache to have me home and well again.

"I brought this for you," my dad said, handing me the purple bunny. "Happy Easter. It's so good to see you." He gave me another hug. Little did I know at the time that this stuffed bunny would become a cherished treasure long into adulthood, reminding me of both the love of my earthly father as well as my heavenly Father.

Awkward hugs were exchanged between each patient and their parents or visitors and then we were ushered to our seats for dinner. They had done their best to make it a special and festive meal. The table had some colorful porcelain Easter eggs atop curly plastic grass. A table monitor sat at each end of the long tables, ready to redirect conversations or behaviors that were deemed unhelpful for recovery. The visitors had met with the lead therapist just before dinner to receive some education and coaching on the dos and don'ts of treatment life.

Honestly, I don't remember what we talked about over dinner. I felt like my parents' jaws dropped wide when they realized I had finished everything on my plate without any tears. Some patients were not able to do this, and the table monitor called the nurse to bring them a cup of Boost to supplement what they refused to eat.

Next on the agenda was chapel time. Unique to this treatment center, which was founded as a Christian treatment center but has since been bought out and converted to a secular facility, patients attended a short chapel service each day. During this time, a group of volunteers would play guitar and sing praise songs and then share a short devotional message. I looked forward to chapel time each day. The presence of God was so vivid, and I was able to break out of my dissociated fog for that half hour as I stood with my hands raised, singing about trading my sorrows and shame without caring that my childlike, off-key voice rang out louder than most. Even in that place of fear, trauma, and confusion, I knew God was with me, and the divine connection I felt worshipping my Creator God was the rainbow of hope that carried me through the storm.

Soon it was time for my parents to return home, and I was once again left behind. Every night, I would hold Purple Bunny tight against my chest as I shut my eyes and attempted to shut out the sound of the Kangaroo pump that was my nightly companion. *They still love me. If I can just do good enough, they will let me come home again. I won't mess up this time. I won't let them send me away again.* Burying my head in Purple Bunny's soft ears I vowed never to let my parents—or anyone else for that matter—down again.

CHAPTER FOUR

LIVING THE LIE

*A*fter three and a half months, I was deemed well enough (either by my treatment team or insurance, or both) to return home. Sadly, many individuals who struggle with eating disorders do not receive adequate time in higher levels of treatment due to insurance cutting them off for arbitrary reasons instead of looking at the whole person and their long-term best interest. In my case, I was too young to go to the step-down care at that treatment facility, so I had to go directly from residential care to home. In an ideal world, a residential patient would be stepped down more slowly and have more than weekly one hour individual counseling sessions when coming home. However, given my age, geographical location, and resources, the best we had was a dietitian from a local dialysis center and a local Christian counselor who had limited training in eating disorders or adolescent counseling. While I met with this "treatment team" regularly, it wasn't what I desired, nor did it bring me to long-term recovery. Nevertheless, I am grateful for the support I did have, even if more would have been ideal.

The hardest part of returning home from three and a half months away at treatment was the feeling that I was living a lie. I don't remember anyone ever explicitly telling me that I could not tell my peers or relatives about what I experienced in Arizona or about my diagnoses or emotions. And yet, I held deep shame about having anorexia nervosa, generalized anxiety disorder, and major depressive disorder at age eleven. I also held a lot of shame around the fact that my family had spent a lot of money they didn't have for me to go to treatment. My relationships with my siblings were strained, my friends from church and co-op seemed to walk on eggshells around me, and I was literally afraid of my own mom and dad. I believed that if I messed up again my parents would immediately send me away. This thought terrified me. I stressed daily over whether or not I was in my parents' good graces and approval.

During my junior high and high school years, I became quite adept at hiding how I was truly doing.

"Yes, mom, I ate the sandwich you packed for lunch." I just left out the part about wiping all the mayonnaise off first.

"How are you, Michelle?" My Sunday school teacher would ask each week.

"Good," I would reply with an unshakeable smile. I certainly was not going to let anyone at church know that I still struggled with feeling depressed and anxious on a daily basis. I had already memorized all the Bible verses about not being afraid and having joy in the Lord. More guilt for my lack of faith was not what I wanted.

"How was therapy today?" Dad would ask. While he probably wanted some hint of hope that I had a new breakthrough and my fears of hot dogs, airplanes, and butter were gone, I would give him a short and simple reply.

"Good," I would say and quickly change the subject. "I am thinking of project ideas for the science fair. Maybe you can help me with it later."

"How did your meal plan go this week? Were you able to do the food fear challenges we talked about last session?" my dietitian would ask when I came for my biweekly weigh-ins at the dialysis clinic.

"Good. I got a donut like we talked about," I would say, telling the truth but leaving out the part about looking up donut calories prior to the outing and making sure I restricted at dinner and snack the night before to compensate for the fear food challenge I was tasked with to prove to my dietitian, family, and the world that I was, indeed, doing good.

The problem with good is that it leaves out a whole lot of details. For one thing, someone who struggles with an eating disorder, depression, anxiety, or other mental health disorders can often look good on the outside while feeling far from good on the inside. Between believing that it was not acceptable to share my struggle with the world and being terrified of being sent back to treatment if I was not doing good, I did my best to maintain this lie throughout my junior high and high school years while living under my parents' roof. This is not to say that I never enjoyed anything or that I was blatantly deceptive, hiding, or lying to my parents every day. My good Christian girl conscience would not allow that. But I did hide enough of my internal struggle to make sure my parents and treatment team would leave me alone for the most part. I ate in front of my family. I went to therapy and my dietitian as prescribed. And my weight remained relatively stable for a while.

My time away at treatment disrupted my sixth-grade year. When I returned, my parents thought it might be helpful to enroll me part time in a private Christian classical school that most of my former homeschooling friends from co-ops were now attending. I got to play volleyball for those two years and enjoyed meeting new people and having different teachers, but I continued to feel like an outsider. For one thing, I only went there one or two days a week for about two hours. For another thing, it felt like I was moving through life as several different persons. At home, I was known as the broken kid who needed mom to tell her what to eat every day and had emotional issues and cried for no reason. At school, I was the smart, quiet kid who only showed up a few times a week and no one really knew much else about her history. At church, I was the kid who had all the right answers, received all the Bible memory awards, and had mysteriously been missing for three and a half months in sixth grade, but no one really seemed to care since she was the homeschool kid who didn't go to movies or the mall or talk about boys or anything cool anyway.

I transitioned to public school in ninth grade and attended Greenwood High School through twelfth grade. Once again, I was the smart kid who turned her work in on time, wasn't afraid to answer questions out loud in class, and strove for academic success without any coaxing from parents or teachers. In fact, I graduated as valedictorian of my class, was in the National Honor Society, and took all the college credit and AP classes I could. I think I somehow thought that if I made good enough grades, my parents would forgive me for my other shortcomings or for how much money all my therapy was costing. Or maybe I hoped that my academic victories would keep everyone distracted from noticing my lack of physical and emotional victory.

I kept going to my therapist and dietitian. Having only played volleyball for two years in junior high and never being particularly good at it, I did not try out for the team in high school. Instead, I played tennis. My dad loves tennis and encouraged all of us to play. It wasn't that he made me play. But, as a people pleaser, I was eager to make him proud. Perhaps more of the reason was that there were no tryouts for tennis. Few people cared about tennis in my high school, so if you were willing to show up to practice and had some sort of racket, you could be on the team. I enjoyed it well enough, but my mind was often elsewhere. When you have an eating disorder, it consumes a *lot* of your thoughts. Instead of enjoying the game or focusing on technique, I was thinking about how many calories I was burning at practice and trying to move my feet as much as possible. My mom would question me about whether or not I was eating enough snacks to compensate for all the calories I was burning. I would assure her that I was, while hoping that I could get away with as few as possible. I remember one of my coaches once telling me that I did not have enough arm strength to be good at tennis. These were the kind of things my parents or others would say when they noticed me losing weight. I was very uncomfortable around that coach after that and felt like he was constantly watching and judging me. Soon after this, I asked to quit tennis.

My parents agreed to let me try cross-country instead of tennis. I have always been a pretty good runner and enjoy running outdoors. While I think many people with eating disorders claim they love to run just because they want an excuse for burning more calories, I truly enjoyed the freedom I felt when out on the open road. That being said, I still was not in tune with my body's needs and feared gaining weight because of how uncomfortable the rapid weight gain had been in treatment. But I was not one of the people who spent hours a day running or working out at the gym. I was satisfied with my one- or two-mile run in cross-country practice with my team, or if it was summer I would run on my own through the empty cotton fields or lease roads around my house.

My first year running cross-country I had a great time and excelled. I was one of the fastest runners on our team—although it was a small team, so that is not saying a lot. I was able to eat enough to fuel my body for the running, and I had fun with the team. We actually made it to regionals that year as a team, and I was known for being the girl who could run long distances in the 100-degree west Texas heat. Unfortunately, I began struggling more my junior and senior year in high school and my running ability suffered. I am not sure what it was that caused me to start relapsing. Maybe it was the fact that I had never really been in true recovery to begin with. While I wanted to be "recovered," I did not know how to make it my own or to do it by myself or for myself. So the more independence I gained as a teenager, the less my mother sat over me at every meal and snack, and the more the voice of the eating disorder was able to sneak in and infiltrate my healthy thoughts with its lies again.

During my junior year, at school I started throwing away part of my lunch, and my weight was dropping again. I was scared of my dietitian appointments because I hated feeling guilt and shame for not meeting goals and being threatened with treatment or stopping sports if I did not quit losing weight. The threat of treatment caused me to water load prior to dietitian appointments to try to keep my team and family from realizing how much weight I had lost or from intervening. Water loading is when you drink a lot of water (about six or seven liters) to flush your body of excess water weight. It's a common tactic in combat sports and bodybuilding for quickly reducing weight to meet specific weight class requirements. But initially it increases your weight because of the amount of water you take in.

One day at practice I downed two thirty-two-ounce Nalgene bottles of water before my mom arrived to pick me up, and I started to see stars. I had eaten a granola bar before practice, so it wasn't from low sugar (or so I told myself). My head felt like it was in another atmosphere. I was dizzy and could not focus, and my head hurt. I was craving something salty. I generally don't like salty foods, but for some reason I wanted all the salty foods and condiments. Somehow, I made it through practice and to my appointment, and the feeling passed eventually. This scared me. On top of the huge weight of guilt for lying to my parents and team, I was stressed about drinking too much water before my appointments.

Looking back, I know that all that water caused my sodium levels to drop dangerously low, which could have caused a fatal seizure or heart arrhythmia. Water is a good thing, but just as with all good things, too much can actually be a bad thing. While I didn't understand the science behind my symptoms, I did start combining my water loading with a good dose of salty pretzels or cucumbers with salt-laden ketchup or mustard or the high-sodium canned green beans, which I claimed as my new favorite snack. By adding extra salt, I was able to chug my two Nalgene bottles of water and not see stars. Of course, I felt nauseous and disgusting, but that seemed a small price to pay to prevent a return trip to imprisonment and nasogastric tube feeding.

I may have fooled everyone throughout my high school days, to some degree. But inside I was crumbling. And my first semester of college was anything but good, and there was no hiding it. I was four hours aways from home, and it became clear that I was a panic-stricken sailor on a stormy sea, trying to hide my fear behind a vast knowledge of nautical terminology.

CHAPTER FIVE

JACKSON FIVE

*I*t did not take long to set up my dorm room, locate all of my classes, and find the cafeteria, and bookstore. There were many on-campus organizations and clubs. I decided to try out the free lunch every Wednesday at the Baptist Student Ministry—although I was not interested in the lunch itself, only the community it offered. I also quickly found a local church to attend and occasionally served in the kid's ministry.

Finally, a chance to be a new person, I thought. *No one has to know that I'm the odd kid who went from homeschooling to private school to public school, mysteriously went missing for three and a half months in sixth grade and returned thirty pounds heavier. Or that I preferred gardening and showing pigs in 4-H to dating or painting nails. I cannot and will not let them know these things. No one will tell me what to choose for lunch in the cafeteria or question me about my emotions.*

To the average observer, I was checking all of the boxes as a freshman in my first semester at college. I had everything under control and running smoothly. I had perfect attendance in my classes, all As, a clean dorm room, and no infractions of dorm life rules. Not one drop of alcohol crossed my lips. I had no overnight parties, and boyfriends were off the table. I was on time to church every Sunday. By all routine measures, I was excelling.

At this point I still believed that my mental health struggles were something to be ashamed of, so I did not open up to my roommate, classmates, advisors, or teachers about my past when I moved to north Texas for nursing school. Considering how I struggled throughout high school and never really made a shift in my eating disorder and still had many depressed and anxious thoughts, it probably comes as no surprise that when I moved away from my parents for college I relapsed quite royally.

It's not that I meant to relapse. But without my mother present to put food on my plate and my therapist and dietitian to hold me accountable to weekly weight checks, I rapidly fell back into old patterns of restricting my intake as a way of feeling safe and numb.

So it is no surprise that when I went home for Thanksgiving break and my parents noticed my anxiety, moodiness, and weight loss, they talked to me about returning to treatment. I felt so defeated. And scared. Terrified is more like it. I was sure that my parents were planning an intervention to send me away to a treatment center again. Between Thanksgiving and Christmas break I worried constantly about what would happen to me when I went home at the end of the semester.

❧❧❧

"We are really worried about you, Michelle," my mom said. "You look so frail. I know you don't want to go back to treatment, but continuing on like you are will lead to . . . well, your heart could stop. I know you think we are just saying that, but it is true. You don't see yourself as sick, but you are. It hurts us to watch you waste away like this." My parents sat on the edge of my bed while I tried to hide my small frame behind a pillow and blanket. These talks were always so uncomfortable. I was once again eleven years old, huddled in the corner of my room with clenched jaw as my mother tried to feed me bananas by hand. I could smell it, feel the carpet under my bony thighs and taste the sickly sweet, gooey banana as I finally opened my lips to allow in the tiniest bite possible.

My dad's voice jolted me back to reality from some space between dissociation and memory lane. "I looked up a place in Dallas," he said. "It is an intensive outpatient program. You would not have to live there. You would just go to groups and therapy and supported meals each day. Almost like college. Since Dallas is too far to commute, we can look at an extended stay hotel or something."

I love my dad. He is a fixer for sure. Give him a problem and he will give you a solution. I did not want to go to Dallas and meet a bunch of new doctors who would tell me everything I had already heard a thousand times about how I was destroying my bones, my muscles, and my fertility. But this sounded like a better option than being locked up in Arizona for months. Perhaps there were no actual locked cells, but a treatment center surrounded by miles of nothing but saguaro cacti is a pretty clever and humane substitute for metal bars if you ask me.

"I guess so," I said. Stuck in a flood of trauma memories, shame, and fear, these were the only words I could form. And so my dad made calls, loaded the car, and drove me to Dallas to check into this supposedly cutting-edge program for eating disorders.

I remember being surprised as we walked into a modern-looking office building that included a Starbucks and some cute boutiques and other random businesses. Inside the suite, however, it was cold and eerie. My dad waited in the lobby while I was ushered into a treatment room and told to sit in a large recliner that reminded me of a dentist chair. The technician hooked me up to some wires and explained that they always start by measuring the basal metabolic rate of the patients to get a feel for their health status and use it to create the most customized meal plan possible. This, I was told, set them apart from other treatment centers.

At least they aren't shoving any food at me . . . yet, I thought. *But I thought the point of recovery was to stop thinking about calories, not to perfect my current obsession with counting calories and calculating daily allowances.*

"Alright, now it is time for your intake with Dr. Walker. He will gather more history and symptoms. Then our whole team will meet to discuss your plan of care, and tomorrow morning we will go over everything with you and give you your treatment schedule and precise meal plan to follow." The technician removed the wires and motioned for me to follow her into an office.

I spent the next few hours answering questions about my family, my eating habits, my emotions, and my physical symptoms. "I feel fine," I said. "No, I'm not tired. I still go running several days a week and have never felt faint or had chest pain. No, I never go a full day without food. No, I'm not a vegetarian. I eat meat." One apple, two handfuls of pretzels, and three cups of coffee in a twenty-four-hour period counts, right? And sure, I eat meat—99% fat-free turkey lunch meat wrapped in lettuce makes a great sandwich.

When the interrogation finally ended, I reunited with my dad, and we checked into the hotel we had booked for the night. I was mentally and emotionally exhausted but could hardly sleep as my mind whirled with anxiety about the next morning. But anything had to be better than cactus prison. Or so I thought.

The next morning my dad and I made our way through Dallas rush hour traffic back to the clinic. Upon entering, I felt a serious tone in the office, and a pit formed in my stomach.

"Good morning, Michelle and Mr. Campbell. Please, have a seat," Dr. Walker said, gesturing toward two straight back chairs across from himself and two other serious looking professionals I assumed to be the dietitian and therapist. "As you know, your condition is rather serious. While we would love to work with you, it is simply not safe to do so on an outpatient level at this time. I've already made a referral to the hospital nearby that has an inpatient unit for eating disorders. You can get stabilized there, and when they feel you are ready, you can return here to work with our team on an outpatient level."

My mind struggled to comprehend what was said. I looked over at my dad. His mouth was half open, and it looked like he might cry at any moment.

What happened next was all a bit of a blur. Dr. Walker gave us instructions to go directly to a nearby hospital, check in through the emergency department, and from there they would admit me to the eating disorder unit for higher level of care until I was deemed ready to step down to outpatient. My brain yelled at me to run. Far. Fast. Anywhere but here. Instead, my dad and I, like on autopilot, carried out the directions since we were shocked and lost for any other options.

At the emergency room check-in desk, my dad fumbled over his words and looked at me. I gave a confused glance back at him and shrugged my shoulders. He ran through the past two days and said, "So, uh, we were sent here to make sure she is medically stable so she can get back into the outpatient treatment program. It's Dr. Walker. He said he put in the referral."

"Sir, this is the emergency department, we don't take referrals. What is the emergency, exactly?" The lady behind the desk paused, but when neither my dad nor I replied, she continued, "Ok, we will get you checked over for medical stability since that seems to be the concern of this Dr. Walker you mentioned. Let me see your ID and insurance, and I'll get you checked in."

Fortunately, at ten in the morning, the emergency department was nearly empty, and we did not wait long before I was called by a nurse to a small room with an uncomfortable hospital bed and told to put on a gown. The nurse checked all my vitals, drew some blood, then left and said the attending doctor would come by to discuss results soon. The word *soon* seems to be relative. After what felt like several hours, a tall man in a white coat entered carrying several sheets of paper.

"Great news! There does not seem to be anything alarming on your blood work. But your blood pressure and pulse are quite low. You don't have a fever. Actually, your temperature is strangely low. And of course, your BMI is concerning. I expect based on your heart rate you are an athlete, so I'm not too concerned." He glanced from his papers to me. "So, what was it that brought you in? Something about anxiety and not weight loss?"

I tried to explain again why I was there. The doctor looked confused. Then my dad jumped in and said that he thought I was supposed to be admitted to the eating disorder unit.

"Oh. Hmm, you must mean the psych unit. They treat all the mental stuff. That's on the fifth floor. Jackson Five we call it. Let me page the team up there and see what their availability is. Wait here." And with that, he turned and left the room.

Finally, the nurse returned to the room with a stack of paperwork and a pen. She put it on the tray table beside me where the leftovers of my sandwich from lunch sat. "Alright, just sign these forms, and we will get you transferred on up to Jackson Five. Here, I'll take your tray while you look over and sign these and will be back in a few minutes." She grabbed the Styrofoam tray with my lunch remains and left me to stare at a pile of forms full of legalese and medical jargon.

Most people might just sign the forms without reading. Fortunately, I knew better than to do that. With my newfound independence as an eighteen-year-old, I was eager to practice my autonomy with informed consent as a full-fledged adult.

Privacy, billing, blah blah blah. But wait, this looks important, I thought. "*You have the right to leave the facility within four hours after you sign a written request to leave, unless the hospital files an involuntary commitment application (see below for information on your rights if you want to leave the facility)." Okay, skip to the below section. "Should the physician deem that you are an immediate danger to yourself or someone else, your request to leave may be denied and further evaluation warranted . . ." Well, I'm not trying to harm myself or anyone else so that won't apply to me. Should be okay to sign the forms, I guess. Not sure what other choice I have at this point. I'm sure after they see I'm stable and willing to eat they will discharge me, and I can go back to the outpatient clinic.*

The nurse returned with a wheelchair and ushered me into it. I told her I'd rather walk. She said it was protocol to use a wheelchair. The closer we got to the fifth floor, the more my anxiety grew. My chest felt tight, and a feeling of impending doom overwhelmed me. When the nurse pushed a buzzer on the wall to request access into the locked unit with large lettering above the door declaring we had arrived at Jackson Five, I wanted to run. An intimidatingly large male nurse in white scrubs appeared out of nowhere.

"I'll take her. Leave the papers on the nurse's desk." Then he glanced at my dad. "No family allowed in the unit outside of visiting hours. You'll have to wait outside." Then he grabbed the handles of the wheelchair. The patient rooms all formed a semicircle around the nurse's desk in the center of the unit. A few doorways stood open, but the nurses at the desk eyed the doorways watchfully. Other doors were shut with a large deadbolt on the outside.

This is worse than cactus prison, I thought. *I have to get out.*

Before I realized what was happening, I found myself in a small room with no windows and only one door that clicked shut behind me. I was alone with the Goliath-like nurse who now held a large blue trash sack.

"Take your clothes off and put them in this sack." He grabbed a clipboard with the outline of a human body drawn on the center. "I need to document all your scars and tattoos." He glared at me. "Come on now. Strip search is standard procedure. I don't have all day. Get it over with."

Slowly, I took off one piece of clothing at a time and put them in the sack. I felt so embarrassed, ashamed, and exploited. At least the last time I was strip searched at age eleven the nurse had been a female. This felt so wrong. He scribbled some notes on his paper as he walked around me to get view of my whole body. I assume he was surprised to see no tattoos or self-inflicted cuts on my wrists or thighs.

"Ok, put on this gown." He shoved a white and blue checkered hospital gown toward me.

"No. I want to leave." The words came out of my mouth without me even realizing what I was saying. "I read in that paperwork I signed. It said that if I sign in voluntarily, I can sign out voluntarily."

"That is not how it works. The doctor on call today will decide that, but we have to finish intake first. You are obviously here for a reason. Voluntary discharge only happens to those who—"

"Are not a danger to themselves or others. Yes, I read the whole thing. I am aware of my rights. I am not crazy. I am here because I was seeking help." I stared back at him resolutely. Where this courage and defiance came from, I still do not know. I believe the Holy Spirit was saving me from further trauma that would have occurred in a locked psych ward. Eventually, the nurse tired of the stare-off and left the room—locking the door behind him—to talk to the physician.

When he returned after what felt like an eternity, he looked utterly disgusted. "Well, I guess the doctor on call today is a softie. He said you can go. Sign here."

I think I must have run out of that room faster than a racehorse out of the gate. In the midst of the ordeal, I had no way of contacting my dad to tell him what had been happening. All the while, he had been waiting outside the Jackson Five ward, frantically calling my mother and trying to figure out what to do. The look on his face was one of relief mixed with desperation. We embraced and all the tears I had not cried up to that point came spilling out.

The drive back to Midland was long. I cried. I called my mom and told her everything that had happened and begged my parents never to make me go to a place like that again. In the end, we all agreed that just returning to college or living at home with bare minimum once a week therapy was not the answer. We also agreed that the Jackson Five locked psych ward was not the answer. After the incident with the intensive outpatient clinic handing me off after one meeting, made us think a higher level of care was the only other option. While I was not thrilled to think about returning to Arizona, I rationalized that a known terror is sometimes better than an unknown one. So I once again packed my bags and headed to the land of Saguaro cacti.

Turns out, it was not as bad as I feared. Being over the age of eighteen, I had more say in the matter. And my parents did their best to empower me to make the decision for myself. I was the one who signed myself into the treatment center this time. Unfortunately, the motivation was still to do recovery for my parents, not for myself. I was able to avoid the traumatizing nasogastric tube feedings for weight restoration, but I still had to endure the highly uncomfortable meal plan. The experience of residential treatment as an eighteen-year-old compared to as an eleven-year-old was extraordinarily different. Groups focused more on processing emotions, learning skills to regulate emotions without using food, and cooking and meal planning. I realized that after my first time to treatment, my mom had done most of the meal planning and prep since I was living at home. She made meals for our whole family three times a day. So when I went to college and had to make my own choices, it was overwhelming and not something I had practice doing for myself. Now, I had the opportunity to learn what it meant to make these decisions without my mom looking over my shoulder or packing my lunch for me.

While I did have to take a spring semester off college, I was able to return again the next fall and finish out my Bachelor of Science in nursing in four and a half years. Those years were filled with a lot of adventure, homesickness, and pushing myself to the limits. I learned a lot about myself. I made friends with a lot of international students, from whom I learned so much about other cultures. I learned to have a greater appreciation for diversity and building relationships. I started meeting with one of the counselors from the university student support center and really grew to enjoy our sessions. She helped me to feel more confident in my ability to make decisions as an adult and gave me space to process the stresses of college life.

I stopped caring as much about what other people thought of me. This led to me opening up with some friends and mentors about my eating disorder and mental health struggles. It was refreshing not to be keeping this big part of my life a secret from everyone. Sharing my struggle and how God remained my source of hope even allowed me to share my faith with some of my international student friends.

And since I wasn't interested in fitting in with the popular crowd, I decided to create my own pseudo sorority called the Phi Nu Kappa (PNK) Piglets. It was basically just me and whatever friends from my dorm or international students who were brave enough or bored enough to join me for whatever silly adventure I planned that week. Sometimes we went to a local park to swing on the swings. Other times we met up to color pictures and write notes of encouragement to slip under people's dorm room doors. We even made t-shirts with the letters PNK and a pink pig face on them.

Speaking of not following the mainstream, I also spent one summer of undergrad in Uganda, doing volunteer mission work in a small orphanage. What an adventure that was! I'm not sure how my parents allowed this. I was over eighteen, so I guess they may not have had any choice. My initial plan was to go on a summer mission trip through the Baptist student ministry. After being turned down due to a history of mental health disorder, which they said was too much of a risk with lack of good care overseas, I did an internet search for my own opportunity. I emailed a contact I found for an orphanage in Uganda and bought my plane tickets.

Looking back, it was a pretty bold move, but I am glad I did it anyway because I learned a lot and grew in my faith and self-confidence. What I did not realize at first is that another nursing student (from a different university) and I would be staying at the orphanage to help care for the twelve kids while the founder/owner and her husband returned to the US for maternity leave.

This meant that two twenty-year-old white girls found themselves shopping at the market weekly for cabbage, carrots, chicken, and beans that the cook, who spoke no English, would cook for all of us each day. It did not take long for us to realize that the prices of cabbage suddenly got higher the moment we arrived at the street market. With some help from the English-speaking "teacher" from the orphanage, who took us under her wing, we learned to haggle quite proficiently. We would say no and walk away if the first price they stated was higher than what we knew to be the going rate. Moments later they would call out with a lower number of shillings to make sure they kept our business even if they could not swindle us into the high prices they tried to charge foreigners.

While I was not fully recovered by any means, during this trip I was able to put the mission and the children first and not focus too much on food fears. I was definitely tired of rice and beans by the end of the two months, but I had eaten what was served and let go of my need to control what and how things were cooked. And I have never been more grateful for hot running water in my shower!

I can understand the concerns of the mission-sending group in not allowing me to go on the organized trip for college students. But they did not even ask more questions or allow me to get a reference from a therapist or doctor. While I am grateful that God opened this other opportunity for me to do summer mission work and believe He worked it all for His good and glory, I'm frustrated and disappointed when religious organizations treat those with mental health concerns as being unfit for mission work. Now having been on six international mission trips and being a professional who understands risk and liability, I believe that further conversation and liability waivers would have been a better way of handling this situation instead of denying me based on my honest answer on a generic application.

The trajectory of my undergraduate years was far from a straightforward path of healing and intuitive living. Academically, I was a model of success. My high grade-point average masked the internal struggle brewing beneath the surface. Physically and emotionally I was slowly unraveling, a delicate tapestry of ambition and exhaustion being steadily pulled apart, thread by thread.

My final semester was a crucible of challenge and complexity. The demanding landscape of my life was an intricate mosaic of responsibilities: rigorous nursing clinicals stretching to twelve hours at a time, part-time tutoring work for the university, and volunteering in international student ministry. I was burning the candle not just at both ends, but seemingly from every possible angle. My inner resources were rapidly depleting.

The semester took an even more harrowing turn when one of my roommates began struggling with severe depression. I'll never forget the moment I discovered her after a suicide attempt, forcing me to make the heart-wrenching call for emergency medical services. Her life was spared, but the emotional aftermath was devastating. In her cultural framework, my intervention was seen as a betrayal, and she resented me for telling her family about her attempt.

Sharing a living space with someone who was both battling suicidal ideation and harboring intense resentment toward you is a special kind of emotional torture. While I cannot attribute my subsequent relapse entirely to this experience, I am acutely aware that such extreme stress does not create an environment conducive to mental health recovery.

As graduation approached, I felt more like a shadow of myself than a celebrant. Graduation festivities, which should have been a time of joy and accomplishment, instead felt like a surreal performance. I was graduating in December because of the missed semester due to treatment, and the impending holiday stress, combined with the oppressive dark winter days only amplified my mental health challenges. Deep within, I was a mixture of desperation, loss, and profound fear about launching a nursing career while feeling so emotionally fragile. It was in this moment of uncertainty that I credit the Holy Spirit with providing unexpected clarity. I knew I needed a different path.

About a week before graduation, I had a pivotal conversation with my mother. Her casual inquiry about graduation party plans was met with my carefully measured revelation: I would be checking myself into residential treatment in Indiana immediately following graduation. Her response was a testament to parental love. Her momentary surprise gave way to unconditional support: "Oh, yes, of course we will support you. Whatever you need."

The subsequent week passed in a blur of transitions: packing my apartment, walking across the graduation stage, bidding farewell to friends and roommates, and booking a flight to Indiana. This time felt different. This was my decision made entirely on my own terms. My parents had not mandated this step, though I suspected they might have suggested it had I returned home.

The autonomy of planning my treatment, making the calls, and choosing the center represented a significant milestone in my journey. It was a declaration of personal agency, a bold step toward taking ownership of my healing process.

Looking back, I recognize this as a profound season of learning. While I cannot claim it was my final encounter with intensive treatment, I can acknowledge the growth and resilience forged during this challenging time. These were simultaneously some of the most difficult and transformative days of my entire life—a complex tapestry of struggle, hope, and incremental healing.

CHAPTER SIX

THE END—ALMOST

I spent that Christmas after graduation in treatment. The residential center attempted to create some holiday spirit by distributing small bracelets with Bible verses and preparing a holiday meal we were required to eat. However, with most therapists on vacation, programming was minimal, leaving us with limited support during an already difficult season.

Months earlier, I had decided to stop taking my Prozac, against medical advice. Medication withdrawals along with stress and malnutrition led to deeper depression, persistent anxiety, and constant obsessive thoughts. My body and mind were struggling, made more complex by the treatment center's approach to my care.

What I now understand as refeeding syndrome, a metabolic condition that occurs when you reinstitute nutrition in people who are severely malnourished, was creating significant physical challenges. My feet and legs became swollen and painful, and I experienced unexpected waves of panic. The residential center, which was not a full medical facility, offered limited medical oversight. When I shared my symptoms, they just suggested I eat less salt or prop up my legs during group.

My metabolism was in overdrive, and the meal plan became increasingly intense. I was required to drink an extra shake before breakfast and take supplements at each of the six scheduled eating times. Each meal felt like an insurmountable challenge, but it was a necessary step in recovery.

There were only two other patients present over the holiday. This isolation made the experience feel even more challenging. During phone calls with my mother, I would often cry, describing how difficult staying in treatment felt. Her encouragement to stay the course, while well-intentioned, sometimes intensified my feelings of guilt and shame.

I found myself caught in a difficult position. Staying felt overwhelming, but leaving would mean disappointing everyone who supported my recovery journey. It was a delicate balance between personal struggle and collective hope for my healing.

I was stuck. With only one way out.

Thirty-six, thirty-seven, thirty-eight, thirty-nine, forty, forty-one, forty-two . . . Forty-two beats in sixty seconds. Still not slow enough, I thought.

I rolled over and pulled the covers up over my ear again, trying to tune out the sound of my roommates' breathing in the other beds, which were spaced equally around the large room. I sighed a bit too loudly and noticed the flashlight beam dance toward my side of the room from the nighttime staff who sat by the door reading a book or scrolling in her phone while she watched us sleep. Being watched in one's sleep may sound creepy to some. It was off-putting to me at first, but by my third time in a residential psychiatric facility, it became a new sort of normal.

God, why can't this all just be over? I thought. *I know I'm not supposed to want to die, but since I don't really feel like this is living anyhow, I think an end to this pain is the most merciful and reasonable answer. The doctor keeps saying there are all sorts of fatal complications I could endure as if that will convince me to magically start eating cheeseburgers and going out with friends and laughing and just being happy—whatever that means.*

Being told your behavior could kill you might convince you to do whatever the doctor said in an attempt to prolong your days on this earth. If only the doctor knew that the fatal ending she warned me of was exactly what I was praying for that night. Unfortunately, my heart refused to stop its rhythmic pulsing, and my body was somehow able to subsist on less than five hundred calories a day and a glucose level less than forty.

A normal fasting blood sugar for an adult is between seventy and one hundred. Most teens or adults with a blood sugar of forty would be passed out. And five hundred calories a day is less than most adults eat in one meal or less than one third of what the body requires just for basic metabolic function. But my body had switched into starvation mode, slowing all bodily processes to conserve energy and breaking down muscle to provide the needed energy just to stay alive in spite of my secret desire not to stay.

Alright, God, I'll give it one more night to let it happen naturally, I prayed. *I beg you to have on me. It's not like I'm doing You any good anyway. If You hear me, if You care, just let this be the last time I fall asleep on this earth. I don't want to take matters into my own hands. I know that would be murder and is a sin, but I literally cannot take it any longer. If I'm still here tomorrow night, I have a plan.*

As if on cue, a train whistle blew long and loud into the night, and I smiled contentedly. I had a plan—and a back-up plan. The railing from the second story balcony certainly felt strong enough to support my weight. That could possibly work if the night staff went on a long smoke break or dozed off. Alternatively, I could sneak to the front door when the staff was distracted by taking another patient to the bathroom and run to the tracks where I'd find a quiet place to lay my head down one last time.

Sorry God, I hope you can forgive me. I am out of hope, out of options, and I have made up my mind this time.

I closed my eyes and tried to block out everything. I slowed my breathing and prayed that God would forgive what I had planned next. Then, an unexplainable presence came over me.

Michelle. It's me.

Who?

I Am.

Oh, sorry.

Why?

Because I'm sure you are mad at me for my horrible thoughts, and I'm a failure and a disappointment to you and everyone else.

Disappointment, by definition, would mean that I had an expectation of you that you did not meet. But since I already know what you have done and will do, I've never had an expectation that you would do anything more or less than what I already know.

I was confused. But also felt great peace. If I couldn't disappoint God, maybe He could still love me despite all my failings. And maybe there was a sliver of hope?

Michelle, if you still have breath in your lungs, I still have a purpose for your life. I will use this—the pain, the tears, the struggle—for your good and My glory. But you have to stay earthside to experience that.

Stay earthside? I wondered. *Oh, I guess He means I can't follow through with what I had planned for tomorrow. But could He still have a purpose for me? Like He could use this broken vessel for anything of worth?*

Ok. I'll try I thought and shrugged wearily.

I know, came the soft, reassuring reply.

And then the voice and presence were gone. But the peace and resolve remained. I knew what I had to do. I had no idea if I would stay in treatment or bail and go home or be sent to a psych ward or excommunicated from my family. But I knew that I would be staying earthside. I chose to trust that God's timing for my life's beginning and end is not for me to dictate. And I rested in the new revelation that I was not a disappointment to God. And that His presence in my life was not reliant on my ability to perform or recover. What was almost the ending became a new beginning.

I wish I could say that I never again struggled with disordered thoughts about food or my body and that my anxiety, OCD, and depression disappeared after that encounter with God. My recovery story is much less straightforward than that. I cannot say that I never again had a suicidal thought or desire. However, I did have a peace and resolve from God that if I was breathing, God still had a plan and purpose for my life and a hope from Him that kept me fighting to stay, even on the darkest days.

PLEASE DON'T MAKE ME BECOME A WOMAN

One art therapy project from this time in treatment still stands out in my mind. I drew a picture of myself, sitting Indian style on the floor, hair long and loose around my shoulders, and a tear escaping from the corner of my eye. The pencil drawing showed the curves of a woman's body, but the posture and poise of a sad and scared child. I had begun to realize that a part of my fear of gaining weight was tied to my fear of becoming a woman.

The internal dialogue of my adolescent days returned to my mind as I gazed at my artwork and prepared to process it aloud with the art therapist and group: *Boys have it so*

much easier. They don't have to worry about covering up their
chests or their shirts being too tight or too low. It's not so bad
when we are young, but as we get older, there are just so many
negatives to being a girl. Periods for one. I can't imagine having
to deal with bleeding every month for the rest of my life! And
then there's all the church talks on modesty and making sure we
aren't leading men into lust and sin by what we wear or how
we act. I can't avoid a tight shirt when my breasts grow and I
need a bra to keep them from jiggling. If I have to be a girl, at
least don't make me become a woman, God.

I can distinctly remember wishing that I had been
born a boy when I was in grade school. My brothers got
to do cool activities like learning to start fires and making
wooden racecars at church while I had to bake cookies
or get dressed up for a daddy-daughter Valentine's day
banquet each year. Had I been born about fifteen years
later, I probably would have been pressured to question
my gender identity or been diagnosed with gender
dysphoria. I am thankful that I did not go down that
slippery slide because I believe it would have just added
to my confusion and pain and list of issues to work
through later in life.

It's hard to explain how I felt inside, but I think a lot
of my disdain for being born a girl revolved around the
fact that I was more interested in playing outside with

cars in the mud than playing princess, and I always feared changes and the unknown, which girls faced way more of in their preteen and teen years. So I figured being a boy would have just eliminated a whole slew of problems.

While I never had a conscious thought that starving myself would keep my body from changing as quickly, since my eating disorder began at age eleven prior to any natural start to puberty, subconsciously understanding that restriction was saving me from becoming the woman I so feared gave my anxiety and anorexia a stronger foothold.

Shame. Perhaps one of my most familiar emotions during these years. I felt ashamed of my wishes not to be a woman, and ashamed of my fuller chest, pubic hair, and touching thighs. Somewhere mixed up in the warnings about abstaining from sins of premarital sex and immodest dress, I had absorbed feelings of shame for just being a woman. While I am positive that this was not the intention of any of my church leaders or parents, young minds internalize words that are often meant for good and turn them into messages of criticism and shame.

❧❧❧

"Michelle, I've noticed you've been having a particularly hard time this week." Even before these words came out of my therapist's mouth, I could tell by the expression on her face and demeanor that an unpleasant conversation was beginning.

Choking back tears I replied, "I'm trying so hard. I'm eating everything—every meal, every shake. But I feel like my body is exploding. I can barely look at myself."

"Well, you are completing your meals, but your emotional resistance to them is concerning. The treatment team and I have been observing your struggles."

"But I'm doing what you ask. Every single bite. Even when it feels impossible. Isn't that what matters?"

"The issue is that you're still fighting the process internally. We need patients who can fully surrender to treatment."

"I don't understand. My behaviors are perfect. I'm following every rule." My voice cracked and the tears began to spill against my will.

"After discussing this with the clinical director, we've decided that an administrative discharge would be appropriate. Your visible distress at meals is disruptive to other patients."

"You're discharging me for struggling? I know I've said I want to leave some days when it is hard and I cry sometimes at meals, but I came here *because* I'm struggling. I'm not trying to not surrender. I don't know what else to do."

"This isn't about your compliance with the meal plan. It's about your attitude. We need patients who can trust us completely and let go of their control issues."

"How am I supposed to just switch off my fears overnight? Isn't this part of the illness? Isn't this why I'm here?"

"I understand you're upset, but the decision has been made. We'll begin discharge planning this afternoon. Perhaps you can find some clarity at home about your motivations or a program that is better suited to treating the level of willingness to engage in treatment." While my therapist offered an outward smile, behind it seemed to be an apathetic stare that said she was just glad to have me off her caseload. Once again, I felt the weight of abandonment and shame wash over me, stirring up all the emotions from my first time in treatment at age eleven. I was a failure. I was too much. I was a burden—a complex patient that no one wanted to take on as their responsibility.

Just like that, my time at the Indiana treatment facility ended. Neither I nor my parents quite understood or agreed with this decision. But it was out of our hands.

I was confused and frustrated and ashamed at that time. Now, when I think about how it all went down, I feel irate! I was completing all my meals and snacks. I was not refusing food; I was not purging secretly or doing jumping jacks in the closet like some of the other girls. As a medical and mental health professional I understand that there are times when someone needs to be referred out to a higher level of care or more qualified treatment for their own benefit. But never should a person be told they are struggling too much or not "surrendered" enough, so they need to just go home and come back when they are ready.

Since it was a "Christian" treatment center, the message I heard was that I was idolizing my food and body over obedience to Christ. I can certainly recognize my sin and imperfection, but I do not believe that eating disorders are in and of themselves sinful or that I was intentionally placing food or body control in a place of higher regard than Christ. I am so grateful that I had the encounter with God a few weeks prior, so I rooted myself in the love and compassion and hope He gave me instead of the shame and condemnation I was feeling by being kicked out of treatment.

CHAPTER SEVEN

PRAYING OUT
MY DEMONS

*B*etween my stays in treatment, I continued to attend church faithfully. I am thankful for the many wonderful supporters and prayer warriors and friends who stuck beside me and my family in the ups and downs. But I also encountered some negative experiences in church that made me reluctant to talk about my struggles.

While church should be a safe place to share about hardships and find support and encouragement, I often felt misunderstood and stigmatized there. Some people really tried to understand. They took time to educate themselves, listen, and provide nonjudgmental love and community. But then there were those who seemed to believe that my years of struggling with mental health and disordered eating was a sign of weak faith. One well-meaning friend referred me to a prayer ministry several hours away. I should have seen the red flag in the price tag, but I was desperate. I did not want to look as if I did not believe in the power of prayer, so I agreed to try it.

I was greeted by a man and wife team who took me into their home—which was where they ran their ministry. Before I really knew what was happening, they were reading from a scripted prayer and directing me to recite after them. While I can't remember all of the words, I know it revolved around confessing sins I was holding onto and renouncing demonic strongholds in my life.

What am I saying? I don't actually think I have a demon inside, I thought. *God, if there is anything you want to show me or that I need to confess or renounce, please show me!*

"What image do you see?" the man asked. "Tell this demon it is no longer welcome. Let the light of God wash over you and penetrate every corner of darkness. Leave nothing hidden." The voice droned on, and I tried to see something, anything that might be the root of evil keeping me from healing. But I saw nothing. I confessed all the sins I could think of—lying to my parents, wasting time thinking about things other than God, asking forgiveness for being anxious instead of just praying and trusting God, and for feeling depressed when I knew I should have joy in Christ. Yes, I was very aware of my sins, but I also knew in my heart that I was not choosing to hold onto my struggles, nor had I chosen to have anxiety, depression, anorexia, or any disorder I was battling.

"What did you see? What image did God give you?" The voice broke through my thoughts again.

Then I saw it, clearly. A tattered and worn, well-loved and misshapen stuffed bunny. *That is how I love you,"* came the still, small voice. *"Like you love Bunny Lou."*

My eyes snapped open. The voice was gone, but the image of the floppy bunny that had been patched to keep the stuffing from all falling out and the ears from falling off remained vivid in my mind. The childhood toy in my mind's eye that I had named Bunny Lou was my favorite stuffed animal. Years of adventures and tea parties outdoors, soaking in my tears on long nights, and trips to more than one treatment center had left it worn, faded, and in need of a full makeover. But I loved it just the way it was. And now God had given me that image as a reminder that He sees me—sees all of His children—just like that. Our scars and imperfections are not hidden from Him, and still He chooses to love us just as we are.

"A bunny. I see an old, bedraggled stuffed bunny," I said as a soft smile started to form, and a tear escaped from the corner of my eye. And that image would continue to be a reminder throughout the years ahead of God's great love and grace for me.

⚬⚬⚬⚬⚬

Whenever I hear a story of "church hurt" that has led to a person rejecting God and hating organized religion, I cringe. While I am sure some people reject God because they take offense at the exclusive claims of Christ being the only way to eternal life, I have heard many stories of people being judged and shamed for their struggles where I believe Jesus Himself would have taken an approach of love and restoration. Jesus loves us too much to leave us in our sin, but He also loves us enough to come to us in the midst of our sin.

Many things people struggle with are not direct results of their own bad or sinful choices. Some mental and physical illnesses can never be boiled down to a single factor. Biology, heredity, trauma, neurological development, socioeconomic factors, privilege, and personality all play a role in mental and physical health. During my darkest days of struggling with anorexia, I confess that I did, indeed, commit many sins of which I am not proud. I lied, hid food, and engaged in destructive behavior toward God's creation, me. Like I said, I am not proud of this, and I have asked God to forgive me. But I also know that much of this was done not as intentional acts of rebellion toward God, but in response to a brain tormented by the clutches of mental illness that led to behaviors I felt I literally had no control over. If you have struggled with an eating disorder or other addiction you probably know what I mean. If you have not, count yourself fortunate, but please do not cast stones at those of us who have.

At some point in my early adulthood, I found out that there were people in my church who questioned my salvation because of my struggles with mental health. When I learned this, I was angry, hurt, and also confused. If enduring struggles were a sign of weak faith, then what do we make of the Apostle Paul saying that he had a "thorn in the flesh"[2] all his life despite repeatedly asking God to remove whatever this was that plagued him? And then we have the story of the man born blind. Jesus's disciples asked who sinned for this man to be blind. Jesus said that it wasn't because of sin that he was blind. Instead, he was born blind in order that the "works of God's might be displayed in him."[3]

Even before my unsupportive prayer ministry incident, I clung to these Bible stories. I prayed for God's healing. Often. But more than that, I prayed for God's glory to be revealed through my life. Even now, as you read this, I pray that you catch a glimpse of the amazing God who created you and who has a purpose for your life just as He does mine. The reason I am writing my story is not to become famous or rich but to bring God glory by proclaiming His wonderous deeds.

If you have church hurt or doubts about the reality and goodness of God, I pray that my story leads you to reconsider. All humans—even church leaders and seasoned Christians—are sinners. I could have let my own church hurt lead me to a bitterness and rejected Christianity or all organized religion. Instead, I chose to root myself in the truth of the Word of God and the Holy Spirit's gentle voice inside that reminds me that I am deeply loved. No matter what. I follow Jesus, not religion. And I engage in a local church that, while not perfect, has proven to imitate Jesus in the way it shows love toward those struggling with mental and physical ailments without casting judgment.

CHAPTER EIGHT

EARLY CAREER CHALLENGES

*S*ince I did not have a job or place to live after graduation and residential treatment, I moved back in with my parents. I am so grateful for their patience and love. Having a roof over my head, good food, and a loving family kept me from fading into despair after the untimely discharge from treatment.

I passed my nursing exam and landed a job at a local community pediatric clinic. Once again I worked with an outpatient team and restarted my antidepressant medication. Having a job provided structure and purpose, and the support of family nearby helped me immensely.

After working in the pediatric clinic for about a year, I wanted to get some experience in hospital. Since my local hospital did not have a pediatric unit, I took a job in an adult ICU step-down unit. It was a radical change of pace! While I was able to work a day shift because this hospital paired new nurses with seasoned nurses for the first year to learn the ropes, I had to work highly stressful twelve-hour shifts, which took a toll on me.

One of my first shifts I had five patients assigned to me. One ended up going into respiratory distress due to ascending paralysis, and the resident doctor on the case refused to listen to my concerns for several hours. Most shifts I stayed at least two hours past shift change to update the charts because there was no time while caring for five near critically ill patients.

I certainly learned a lot during the year I worked there, but eventually the absence of proper meals, high stress, and poor sleep led to my weight dropping dangerously low again. I recognized my need for a higher level of care and resigned from my position. While I had been seeing a therapist and dietitian during this time, I was not being completely honest with them and was not in a strong enough place to balance the stressful job and long hours with staying in recovery. My anxiety and depression were back in full force and my go-to coping mechanism—controlling my food and weight—had stepped right back into place.

Once again, I admitted myself to a residential treatment center and went through the steps of weight restoration, attending group sessions, and meeting individually with a therapist to work on underlying causes. Unfortunately, as with many of the larger treatment centers, it felt like a cookie-cutter approach. At least the medical care exceeded my last stay, and I avoided any refeeding complications this time. My family was again encouraging and supportive; my sister even came to visit me several times since the center was located near her new home. To this day, I am friends with the roommate I had there and God allowed me to play a role in leading her to a saving personal relationship with Christ.

My therapist introduced me to Acceptance and Commitment Therapy, a model I found very helpful. The basic idea is to identify your own personal values— what is most important to you in life—and then to ask yourself if the choices you are making daily are bringing you closer to or further from these values. It helped me shift my perspective from seeing caloric restriction as a bad thing I needed to stop doing to an action that was not bringing me closer to my values of faith, family, serving others, and independence.

As I made progress at the center I gained privileges. I was given passes to leave by myself for short periods of time. The environment, however, was rather toxic at times, which led me to decide to discharge before my team believed I was ready. This center was coed, and there were a few times a male patient made the girls uncomfortable. Also, there were several patients who were labeled *chronic* and had been in and out of this center multiple times. One of them wound up getting committed by her parents.

At the time I had no idea having your free will removed from you because your parents or a doctor deems you a danger to yourself was even a possibility! Watching my peer be legally bound to stay in the treatment center against her own will terrified me. If there was one thing I could not stand, it was the thought of being held somewhere against my will and forced into treatments against my will. It would be a repeat of the treatment stay and nasogastric feeding at age eleven. Now, as a parent and professional, I can understand that this would sometimes seem necessary for the wellbeing of the person, but back then I lost all trust in this center and made a case to my team that I was choosing to discharge early but promised to get involved in outpatient treatment and support groups. I prayed so hard before I met with the psychiatrist who would sign off on my discharge. Since I had stayed and complied with weight restoration for nearly two months by this time, I was not in a physically dangerous place, nor was I suicidal or homicidal. So they had to allow me to leave; and that is what I did.

Once again, transitioning back to caring for myself came with many challenges. I decided to stay in Colorado, where I had gone for treatment, because the bigger city offered more options for outpatient treatment providers specializing in eating disorders. Since my sister and cousin lived nearby, I had some family support in the area. Graciously, my cousin allowed me to rent a room from her in her condo, and I called this home for the next six months.

Since I had resigned from my job before going to treatment, I had no job and, thus, little to occupy my time during the day. There are only so many hours one can fill with appointments, a few free support groups a week through a local nonprofit, and filling out job applications. After the stress of my last hospital job, I decided that it was best for my recovery to look for a nursing job in a clinic or outpatient setting, so I would not have twelve-hour shifts that had contributed to my most recent relapse. Unfortunately, these nursing positions are hard to come by for a nurse with limited experience and no connections in a new state.

The cold, snowy weather and short days did not help my depression, and my anxiety was once again at an all-time high due to having no income, few friends, and unfamiliar church. I had too much time on my hands to get stuck in my head. During the day I would go on long walks around the neighborhood and parks while listening to podcasts or worship music. When the sun went down an intense panic would fall over me. I would cry, often to the point of hyperventilating. Often, I would call my mom, but then spend most of the time apologizing for being such a pathetic daughter before saying goodnight and trying to force my brain to shut off so I could sleep. The pure exhaustion of an hour or more of crying usually allowed me to fall asleep, only to be tormented by nightmares about being locked in treatment centers against my will or being abandoned by my family.

Eventually I got a part-time job at Starbucks just to make some money and fill time while continuing to apply to every daytime nursing job I could find that did not require long hours or critical care. Every day, I fought the urge to drive home to Texas. My mom would often encourage me to stick it out a little longer, knowing that if I gave up too quickly, I would feel all the more like a failure and blame myself for not trying harder. But by six months we both could see that things were not getting any better, and it was taking a toll on my health and weight again. As usual, my eating disorder stepped in to offer a feeling of safety through false control when the rest of my world felt completely out of my control. It was disappointing to have to leave my therapist and dietitian and support group and return to Midland, a place that had little professional support in comparison. However, it was a relief to be back near my parents and the comfort of my hometown.

The way my parents always welcomed me back home but also made sure I was seeing the appropriate professionals so as not to enable me to stay sick is what kept me alive and fighting all those years. They read books, did research, and learned as much as they could about how to help and support me. For that, I am forever grateful. I have since come to know many people who struggle with eating disorders and or other addictions and mental disorders whose families gave up on them after their first or second relapse. Perhaps my parents wanted to give up on me numerous times, and I would not have blamed them, but I thank God that they stuck with me and believed in me when even I did not believe in myself.

Back in Midland, I took a job at another pediatric clinic. After some time, I moved in with a roommate, gained more confidence and independence, and became more settled in my career. Still not in full recovery by any means, I counted calories in my head and weighed myself daily to make sure I did not gain too much weight (though I told my team and parents I was weighing myself to make sure I did not lose weight). The hours and lower stress of the pediatric clinic job and the joy I have when working with kids helped me to find some solid footing for several years.

After I worked a few years at the clinic, a school nurse position opened. I saw it as an opportunity to have summers off to go on more mission trips, so I applied and got the job. While working as a school nurse I went to India twice and then Cambodia, doing medical and orphan care work. I feel truly blessed that God allowed me to have these experiences. I had a short season of sailing on smoother seas before another storm hit, and I had to choose again whether I would give up in desperation and defeat or choose hope and life.

CHAPTER NINE

THE THREAT

*A*few more years into my nursing career, I needed residential treatment yet again. This would be my fifth time (not that I was counting). I had been functioning for years in a malnourished state, but eventually it took its toll and my body and mind were struggling to keep up with full time work, mission trips, and exercise. Stress, illnesses (which are unavoidable when working as a pediatric nurse), and being inconsistent with seeing my therapist and dietitian eventually caught up to me.

I once again knew I needed to seek more intensive help. My dietitian insisted that I needed some further medical testing and referred me to an eating disorder specialist five hours away. Reluctantly, I drove to the appointment, expecting to be told I needed to gain some weight and lay off exercise for a while. But this doctor was a bit more thorough and knowledgeable than your general practitioner. While I tried to play it cool and say that I had just gotten to a low point after a recent bout of influenza but would bounce back soon, he could see through my attempts to minimize the severity.

"We are going to need to do an EKG to look for any abnormalities in your heart rhythm. A potentially lethal side effect of malnutrition is heart arrythmia," the doctor explained. Then he left the room. The nurse came back in and put ten stickers all over my body, connected them to cords, and waited for a machine to capture the electrical pattern of my heart on paper.

God, please let it be normal, I prayed. *I promise, I'll start eating more. Today. On the way home even. I just can't leave a job one more time and go to treatment.*

Obviously, bargaining with God like this does not usually work, but I was desperate, and my desperate, self-centered plea reflected that.

"It was normal, right?" I asked the nurse as she tore off the sheet of paper and began unhooking me from all the cords and stickers.

"Oh, I can't interpret it. The doctor will review it and then come back in and talk to you about it. You can change from the paper gown back into your clothes when I leave, and he will be in shortly."

I waited in the eerie silence. The room was cold. I was always cold. But I would never say this out loud. I could not stand having one more person say "you just need more insulation" as they patted their well-padded thighs and gave a condescending glance at my small frame.

Finally, the doctor entered the room and took a seat in a chair opposite me, beside a desk with a computer. He pierced me with his eyes and any last shred of confidence I had disappeared like the last grain of sand through an hourglass. Glancing down at some papers he held, he spoke in a stern and serious tone. "Your BMI is dangerously low; your basal body temperature indicates that your body is in a state of mere survival due to insufficient caloric intake. You have bradycardia which tells me your heart muscle has wasted along with the rest of your muscles, leaving you particularly vulnerable to a fatal heart arrhythmia at any moment. Frankly, you should be in a hospital right now receiving intravenous nutrition."

Where is the nearest door? I thought. *This man is going to imprison me. No, I can't let him. I have to hold it together and talk my way out of here. I never should have come. I knew he was going to be extreme and blow things out of proportion. After all, it is his job. He probably gets paid by the hospitals or treatment centers to send people there. He thinks I am just like all the others, but I'm not. I can do this on my own. Treatment only makes things worse because it is such a false reality.*

He paused and stared at me. I did not know if he was expecting me to start crying or agree with him. Before I could decide what to say, he continued, "I understand you are a nurse, so you must understand the severity of the situation and the danger you are putting your patients in each day. Someone in your state is incapable of critical thinking and fast decision-making, not to mention the physical stamina required to care for patients who are counting on them."

As if that settled the matter, he handed me a brochure with a picture of a girl and a horse on the front. It said, "Avalon Hills: Treat to Outcome."

"I highly recommend this treatment center. They can accommodate those in fragile medical conditions like yours and have a model unlike any other. They keep the patients until they are doing well both physically and mentally instead of discharging them too soon as is the case at so many centers that are driven only by insurance-demanded, short-term cures. I can have the nurse give you a form to sign so I can send the referral. Their intake team will call you by the end of the week." He typed some notes on his computer as I stared numbly at the brochure in my lap.

So, this place makes people stay until their team decides they can leave? No way, I am NOT going to this place. Who cares about the horses and sprawling acres of green grass. Prison with a facelift is still prison. Sounds like a one-way ticket to giving up all free will to me.

"Um, thanks. It looks like a lovely place, but I have already made plans to increase the frequency of my appointments with my therapist and dietitian at home and found some online support groups I will start attending. I have been to residential treatment already and learned a lot, but the purpose I get from working and staying connected to the real world is what helps me to make lasting changes."

"I don't think you understand. Of course, most people at your state are in strong denial. This is not optional, Michelle. If you refuse to go to treatment, I may need to make a report to the board of nursing about your endangering your patients." He stopped typing and his eyes shot straight to my soul.

The tears flowed. I could not stop them now. "I am not refusing treatment; I just need to look over my options and talk to my parents about insurance and all that. Thank you for your time. I'll talk it over with my team."

"I'll be sending a message to your team with my recommendations as well. They would be foolish to continue seeing you on an outpatient level in your state. You are a walking liability. If you don't act quickly, a heart attack will make the decision for you, and an ICU bed is much less comfortable and enjoyable than equine therapy with a supportive community of peers." He closed his laptop, stacked his papers on top of it, and stood up. "I'll be calling you and your therapist in two days to see which treatment center you decide upon, so I can send over my referral and notes. I really should not be letting you walk out of here alone. Do you have someone who can give you a ride? It would not be safe for you to be behind the wheel of a vehicle given your—"

"I can call my parents. I have friends and family nearby." I stood up and beat him out the door. Before the office door closed behind me, my eyes were full of tears, and I was gasping for breath between sobs of anger and panic. I walked as fast as I could to the parking lot. I had no intention of calling anyone for a ride. Who did this man think he was? God? How dare he threaten my nursing license! How dare he treat me like a child! As flashbacks of a nasogastric tube being forced down my nose and throat as an eleven-year-old clouded my memory, I vowed to not let this man or anyone take my independence from me ever again.

FIVE WEEKS OF SOLITARY CONFINEMENT-ISH

Before even stepping into the specialist's office, I already knew deep down where I was headed—back into treatment. There's a point in relapse where something inside me shifts, like a switch flipping, and I know I can't climb out of the hole on my own with just outpatient care. Still, I wasn't going to dive in blindly this time. After more than one negative experience in residential treatment, I felt a mix of anxiety and dread at the thought of going back. But the truth was undeniable: I'd been trying to make changes on my own for months, and things had only gotten worse. It was time to face the reality I'd been avoiding, to admit to myself, my family, and my treatment team that I needed more support.

Unfortunately, my initial options were limited by my compromised physical state. Residential treatment centers usually require a medical evaluation showing that the person is stable enough not to require frequent medical monitoring or a physician on site at all times. Based on my abnormal EKG, low BMI, and borderline bloodwork numbers, the residential treatment centers I was interested in were unwilling to take me until I was deemed "stabilized" by an inpatient (or hospital) treatment center. Thus, I decided to go to an inpatient hospital unit that specialized in eating disorder medical stabilization. From there I would transition as quickly as they would allow to a residential center where more of the actual therapy would occur.

I'm sure it won't take more than a week for them to see that my heart is stable and that I am willing to eat. I'll just pack a few books and journal to keep me occupied until I get to the residential center, where the schedule is always full of groups, individual sessions, cooking challenges—and if I'm lucky—some time for art and yoga. I'll do my time and prove to them that I am motivated and ready to work hard for recovery.

It is a good thing I did not know ahead of time that I would spend five whole weeks in that one small hospital room by myself. Had I known, I am sure I would have refused to go. Only by God's grace and strength did I make it through those five long weeks—one day at a time. Each day I met with the doctor I would tell them I was ready to transition; each day they would tell me that either my bloodwork was not yet stable or my BMI was too low.

For the first week, I wore a continuous heart monitor. A nurse's aide sat by my bedside 24/7 for the first three weeks. Sitting still has never been an easy task for me. This was the biggest test of my patience yet. Some days I just stared at the blanket pulled over my feet and legs as I sat semi-reclined in the adjustable hospital bed. I would trace the pattern on the blankets with my fingers and watch the clock—waiting for time to pass. After a few days of this, and realizing that I was not going anywhere fast, I decided to try to keep my mind occupied.

Focusing on books is difficult when malnourished, so I listened to worship music on my phone while crocheting. It did not take long for me to run out of yarn. Fortunately, my mom was willing to ship me more yarn, and I dove into crocheting little animals as if my life depended on it. In a way, it did. The nurses and aides started to be quite intrigued by my crocheting. They would ask me what I was making and then even requested specific animals. Pinterest became my best friend. Using free patterns or sometimes just pictures of what I wanted to make, I soon had a zoo of small, crocheted animals.

I cannot say that I *enjoyed* my time in the hospital, but by God's grace I came out of it a better person. Day by day I grew in patience, humility, and compassion for my body. Instead of falling into despair from boredom and isolation, I sought purpose in being a light to the nurses and aids and doctors caring for me. Since patients were in individual rooms, I could not interact with other patients on my unit except for when occasionally a nurse would wheel me in a wheelchair to the hospital courtyard for fresh air. I left encouraging quotes beside my crochet animals on the nurse's station so other patients could see them and be encouraged as they passed by. As awkward as it is to eat three meals and three snacks alone at a table with a monitor watching from across the room, I made the best of it and would make small talk or listen to music. A handful of worship songs comforted me through many a long hour in that hospital, and Scriptures I had memorized as a child brought peace when anxiety and depression threatened to derail my will to keep going.

Since many of the other patients in the unit were not physically or mentally well enough to engage in therapy, the medical staff did not offer group therapy, only two thirty-minute sessions with a counselor each week. I would have loved to get more counseling and therapeutic work during this time. To make use of my time, I listened to a lot of recovery-oriented podcasts while crocheting and looked forward to the deeper therapy work to come. Finally, the day came when I was allowed to transition to a residential treatment center.

❧❧❧❧

My heart quickened and I held my breath. I could hardly believe I was stepping out of the building that had been my home for the past five weeks. I sat with anticipation in the back seat of a large taxi, drumming my fingers on my thighs as I waited for the driver to leave the parking garage of the hospital. My next stop was the Denver airport, where I would get on a plane to St Louis. From there another taxi was lined up to ferry me to the treatment center that sat in a secluded neighborhood outside of the city. The sights and sounds around me were exhilarating but also overwhelming after having been isolated from the masses and sheltered from the cacophony of lights and noise of our modern, fast-paced society.

It's not too late to back out. Switch your flight. You can be back in control. Don't eat anything at the airport. Walk as much as you can before your flight boards. Why not rent a car and just drive back to Texas. Or maybe somewhere new? Start over. Why are you willingly subjecting yourself to another stint of incarceration?

The thoughts darted about in my mind like tiny fish in an aquarium, refusing to be caught. I knew well enough by now that these were what my therapist would refer to as "ED thoughts." Thoughts rooted in the eating disorder (ED) and not my own. They sure felt like my thoughts after so many years heeding their warnings and advice. How could they not be mine? It's not like

I read them somewhere or watched them in a movie. But that is the thing about mental illness. It hijacks the rational side of the brain and replaces it with obsessions and compulsions that are usually not rooted in truth or reality.

"Shut up!" I didn't realize I had said it out loud until the person sitting next to me at United Airlines gate B 34 gave me a questioning side glance. "Uh, sorry. Not you. Just got lost in my thoughts." My right foot started shaking nervously as I tried to still my mind and avoid eye contact with anyone. I glanced at my watch. Still forty minutes until boarding. Time for another lap around the concourse.

God, please take away these ED thoughts. I know where they lead. I can't give in now. The very fact that they are so loud when I am given one day of freedom to make my own decisions is why I know I need to follow through with the rest of treatment. Obviously, I am not strong enough yet to be on my own and maintain recovery. As much as I want to be free to eat what I want, drive my own vehicle, hang out with my friends back home, hug my mom, feel purposeful by working in my career again, the truth is a life enslaved to food rules, irrational anxieties, and dark waves of depression are threatening to sweep me under for good. Oh, God, I wish you would just give me a new brain! I am so tired of fighting.

What if I go through all these months of treatment again and then relapse? Is this just a waste of time and money? I can't disappoint my family, myself, and You again.

"You can't disappoint me," came that still small voice once again. "But you have to keep fighting."

Tears welled in my eyes, and I looked up to see that I had walked all the way back to the food court in the main concourse without realizing I had even left my gate.

Okay, God. I'll keep fighting. But only if You help me.

Just then one of the Bible verses I had memorized in the hospital surfaced through my mental fog: "The Lord will fight for you; you need only to be still" (Exodus 14:14 NIV).

I thanked God for bringing His word to mind right when I needed it. Suddenly, I became aware of my stomach growling as I inhaled the aroma of hot grilled chicken and vegetables sizzling in silver chafing dishes waiting to be ladled into Saturn-sized tortillas. I knew what I needed to do. With that, I confidently stepped into line, ordered a full-scale nourishing lunch my dietitian would be proud of, and marched back to Gate B 34. It was time to finish what I had started.

CHAPTER TEN

MEETING MY INTERNAL FAMILY

$\mathcal{T}$he next chapter of treatment was, by no means, easy. However, it was refreshing to engage daily with other patients who had much in common. We dug into hard topics in therapy groups and individual counseling, and got hands-on practice with cooking alongside the chefs and dietitians. Each night we all eagerly waited for our bedroom doors to be unlocked so we could pull on pajamas and go to sleep.

Therapy is exhausting. The mental and emotional energy expended in treatment centers is on par with the physical intensity of an Olympic training center. If you have experienced this level of fatigue, you know what I mean. If not, be glad you have not needed this type of intense work to rewire faulty brain circuitry that has upended your life and health.

While this was my fifth time in residential treatment, something was very different this time. Yes, it was a different location. Yes, I had a different treatment team. Yes, I was partially relieved just to be out of a hospital bed. But there was more than that. Something inside me had shifted. Like the ropes that had tied me so tightly to rigidity and fear had loosened a bit, and I was starting to experience life in a whole new light. There was laughter. Hope. Peace. Instead of obsessing every moment about when I would get to leave and how many calories were in the meals and instead of questioning if the dietitian was secretly trying to make me fat, I connected to the other patients and peeled back the layers of my past trauma and wounds.

Unlike the other treatment centers and therapists, this one utilized a therapeutic model called Internal Family Systems (IFS), developed by Richard Schwartz. IFS therapy views our inner world as made up of different parts, like sub-personalities that develop to help us cope with life experiences. Some parts act as protectors, trying to keep us safe through controlling behaviors while others might react like firefighters, rushing in with impulsive actions to extinguish emotional pain. In eating disorders, these parts often manifest as the voice that drives restriction, overexercise, or other harmful behaviors. The genius of IFS lies in its compassionate approach to these parts, understanding that even destructive behaviors originally emerged as attempts to help or protect. While it seemed odd and almost mystical at first, I came to realize it as a key instrument in my lasting recovery.

"I'd like to try exploring something a bit different today," Jaimie, the primary therapist assigned to me said. "I'm wondering if we could get curious about these different parts of you that you've been experiencing." Jamie was warm and engaging, easy to talk to, and had an office with a nice window, allowing natural light to fill the small room.

"You mean like my anxiety and the eating disorder?" I replied. "I just wish they would go away. They make everything so hard."

"I understand wanting them to go away. What if I told you that these parts—even the eating disorder—originally came about as a means of trying to *help* you cope with difficult experiences?"

I raised my eyebrows skeptically. "*Help* me? But all they have done is interrupt my life and cause harm."

"They can absolutely cause harm now. But often these parts develop when we're younger and are trying to protect us the only way they knew how. Like your perfectionism. It might have developed as a way to help you feel safe and in control when things felt really chaotic."

I paused thoughtfully. "I never thought about it that way. My last therapist just kept telling me to fight against these parts of myself."

"Instead of fighting them, what if we get curious about them? For instance, we could ask your anxiety part what it's trying to protect you from. Or thank your eating disorder part for trying to help you cope, even though its methods ended up causing pain."

"That feels . . . different. Less like I'm at war with myself. But how do we actually do that?"

"We can start by just noticing when these parts are present and speaking to them with compassion. Like when you feel that anxious part rising up, you might say 'I see you're trying to keep me safe right now. What are you worried about?'"

I teared up a bit, imagining ending the war within myself. "That's so different from how I usually talk to myself. I'm usually pretty unsympathetic with these parts of myself. I feel like they are bad and need to be banished."

Jaimie smiled warmly. "Yes," she said, "and beneath all these parts is your core Self, what you beautifully described as your true, God-given self. This Self has natural compassion, wisdom, and the ability to heal."

"I can feel that. When I'm really quiet sometimes. Like there's a peaceful part of me that knows who I really am."

"Exactly. And from this Self, we can learn to be curious about and care for all your parts, even the ones that have been using harmful strategies like the eating disorder."

"This makes so much sense with my faith too, like seeing the real me as something good and whole even when these other parts are struggling. And not hating any part of myself."

"Yes, and as we help these parts feel heard and understood, they often relax their grip on their extreme strategies. They don't need to shout so loud to get your attention."

"I've spent so long fighting against myself. This feels . . . gentler somehow. Like maybe recovery isn't about destroying parts of myself but understanding them."

"Exactly. It's about integration rather than elimination. All your parts, even the eating disorder, were trying to help you survive. Now we can help them find new, healthier ways to support you."

"For the first time, I feel like maybe I can heal without having to hate myself in the process." A new glimmer of hope began to form inside me that maybe this time in treatment would lead to long-lasting recovery.

"That's such a powerful insight. Would you like to practice speaking to one of your parts right now, with my support?" Jaimie leaned forward in invitation.

"Yes, I think I'd like to try talking to the anxiety part. It's been really loud lately with all the meal plan changes," I replied.

"Beautiful. Let's start by just noticing that part with curiosity and compassion and see what it might want you to know," she said, making it sound so simple.

It did not feel simple at first, but over time it became a regular part of my internal dialogue—one that I still use to this day and now am able to teach to my own clients. What I gained at this last treatment center was much more than just pounds. I gained a sense of Self like I had never known before: laughter, confidence, and a renewed hope and passion for life. I learned to talk to myself—my inner parts—with empathy, compassion, and curiosity. Instead of getting bogged down in a cycle of shame every time I let anxiety overtake me or an eating disorder behavior derail my progress, I learned to stop and notice. Usually, there was some stressor-stuffed emotion that needed attending to. Once I took the time to recognize why the part had felt the need to step in and manage or protect in that instance, I could work on the underlying issue and then ask the part to sit to the side, so my healthy Self could be in the driver's seat again.

After about two months I was able to step down to the center's partial hospitalization program (PHP) where I shared an apartment with three other girls and went to groups and sessions and shared meals during the day. Over time, I would be given more privileges to eat some meals on my own at the apartment. This was extremely helpful as a bridge to going home. Every other time in residential treatment I had not been able to take the step-down approach due to insurance coverage or other reasons.

Now I see this as a crucial piece of the recovery puzzle for myself and many others. It is a shame that many insurance plans do not cover PHP or intensive outpatient program programs or that by the time a person is ready to transition from residential they have run out of time or finances to receive proper step-down care and land right back into the grind of full-time work and home life with one therapy session a week if they are lucky. While I do not believe it is good or helpful to force someone to go through all levels of care, I do see my role as a therapist to strongly recommend it for clients and to explain the risks of going straight from residential to outpatient level of care.

Mental health and medical professionals should be aware of and well versed in talking to their patients about the benefits of all levels of care and help them navigate the best path for their individual recovery. And insurance companies ought to seriously consider their models of coverage for different levels of care. Inpatient and residential treatments often are covered almost completely because they fall under "medical" benefits, but lower levels of care, including visits with a therapist, are often not covered at all. If preventive care is supposed to be covered at 100 percent, why could this not include preventive appointments such as seeing a therapist or dietitian as recommended by a comprehensive treatment team?

Too often, individuals like me find themselves cycling in and out of residential treatment centers, emergency rooms, and crisis units because they cannot afford or do not have access to the care they need after being discharged. I do not know how to reform healthcare, but I sure have a few ideas that I think could help patients like my past self to live more stable lives and not live in a chronic state of mental illness and hospital cycling for seventeen years.

THE TATTOO

"So I've been thinking about getting that wave tattoo we talked about," my friend Kimberly said as we sat together on the couch in our shared PHP apartment a few days before my scheduled discharge. "Something about the ocean just feels right, you know? How it's both powerful and peaceful."

"I love that idea! The waves imagery is perfect— how they're always in motion, always changing but still beautiful. Have you thought about where you want it?"

"I'm thinking on my side, not too big, but on my ribcage. What about you? Are you still thinking about 'set free'?"

"Yeah, I am. My parents have always been really against tattoos, though. I've kind of let that hold me back." Truth be told, I had a memory of my father saying, "If you ever come home with a tattoo, you will need to find somewhere else to sleep." But since I didn't live under his roof anymore, I figure maybe I am safe. With a long sigh, I continued, "And honestly, there was a part of me that was scared to get it because I thought, 'What if I relapse?' Then it would just be this permanent reminder of failure."

Kimberly leaned forward and asked softly, "But you don't feel that way anymore, right?"

"No, I don't. I'm ready to claim this freedom for myself. That verse, 'if is for freedom that Christ has set us free' is about so much more than just recovery. It's about becoming who I truly am, making my own choices. Living free from the shame of struggling for so many years, believing that God is not disappointed in me."

"I can relate to that, for sure. It's like the tattoo itself is an act of trusting yourself. I like having a constant reminder of what I have learned and how I have changed," she said, with a resolute smile and nod.

I nodded. "Exactly!" I said. "I'm not the same person I was when I started this journey. I'm stronger now. And even if things get hard sometimes, this will be a reminder of who I really am—not just someone in recovery, but someone who's truly free."

"Have you decided where you want yours?" Kimberly asked as she resumed browsing Pinterest for ideas of wave tattoo designs.

"I'm thinking on my wrist, where I can see it every day," I said. "A daily reminder that I chose this path for myself, not for anyone else."

"It's beautiful seeing you own your story like this. Daria has an artist in town she has used in the past and recommends. Should we call to make an appointment? We only have two more nights together before you head back to Texas."

"Yes! Let's do it. No more waiting to embrace full freedom."

∾∾∾∾

I got the tattoo, was successfully discharged on good terms, and excitedly returned to Texas and my job in school nursing. I resumed working with my outpatient therapist and dietitian and spent time with my family, friends, and church group. My roommate was very supportive and understanding. I felt comfortable talking to her about my experience and being open and honest about my struggles and victories. Having a supportive community is such a vital part of a successful recovery.

The voices of anxiety, depression, and disordered eating still existed and gave their opinion on how best to handle the stress of reentering the real world, but my core Self now emerged as the stronger voice.

You know people are going to comment. They will say "you look so healthy" and ask where you have been. Just don't go. Avoid the comments and questions.

Faithful old anxiety let me know its concerns as I got ready for the young adult Bible study. I had attended regularly prior to going to treatment this go round, but this would be my first time back since being away for two and a half months and gaining twenty-plus pounds. Reentry pains after discharge are a common theme. People aren't trying to be rude or triggering, but they often say all the wrong things or say nothing at all and neither is particularly helpful. Still, avoiding social settings and old friends did not feel congruent to living a life of freedom. With my new mantra—I am set free and will live accordingly—I sat anxiety down for a little chat.

Hey, I get it. It is going to be awkward. You want to warn me about the discomfort and potential embarrassment and triggering statements I'll face if I go. Thank you for your concern, but I am still going.

Unsatisfied with my answer, the eating disorder part piped up with its perceived solutions as well: *Why don't you skip breakfast? That always helps quiet anxiety down! Gives you that 'I'm in control' feeling, and the confidence will make it easier to face the masses. Plus, they often have snacks, and you will want to be able to eat some to show them you are better, so skipping breakfast is not breaking your meal plan per se, just, um, adjusting a bit.*

I sigh. So typical. I've heard this one before. Many times. And in the past, I would have used these suggested strategies to manage anxiety and feel in control. *Look, I hear you. That has worked in the past—for years, in fact. But it comes with some pretty detrimental side effects. I've got to use other ways of coping with my emotions that don't include hurting my body and trying to numb out all the emotions I have considered bad. Emotions aren't good or bad. While all emotions are valid, they are not always based on valid facts. Yes, I am feeling nervous about seeing old friends again. But the anxiety won't kill me. Avoiding going this time won't make it any easier next time. I can't control what others think or say so worrying about it is not helpful. And either way, skipping breakfast won't get me closer to a life of freedom. Using food to feel in control may feel good for a moment, but I know I'll only feel worse later when the guilt and shame set in—not to mention the low energy and brain fog. So, anxiety and eating disorder parts, once again, thank you for your concerns and desire to help me, but I'm going to have to ask you to sit down and busy yourself elsewhere today. Let Self navigate the ship.*

Over the next several months I would have many of these conversations among my internal parts. It didn't feel so weird anymore. Really, I think most everyone can relate to having different "voices" inside their heads that correspond to different drives, agendas, or motives. One voice says to get up and go to work. The other voice says that work is pointless and your boss is a jerk so just stay in bed and binge-watch Netflix. Or perhaps you have a part that seems to parrot everything your mother said to you as a child. This part may be trying to protect you from the glaring look you always got when you fell out of her good graces. Often these parts are stuck in a previous decade—unable to shift to present-day when you are an adult and your mother lives five hundred miles away.

Noticing the different parts with compassion and curiosity and then taking time to recognize what they are concerned about and what they are trying to accomplish is the daily work of self-therapy using IFS[4]. I read books, watched videos, and learned all I could about how to utilize this therapeutic model. It had been so helpful at the latest treatment center, and I wanted to keep myself on a path of recovery. Through my commitment to understanding myself, nurturing my wounded inner child, and following through with appointments with my outpatient team, I was able to stay on track, feel successful in my nursing career, and even have my first boyfriend. There is no denying that God was with me through these years of early recovery. He gave me strength and provided good friends and a supportive family. Anxiety and depression and the eating disorder never left, but that, I learned, was not the goal. Instead, the goal was to embrace all of these parts of me with gratitude for their desire to help me, but then strengthen my core adult Self to now make the decisions and choose healthier coping mechanisms in the face of life's stresses.

CHAPTER ELEVEN

NEW HORIZONS

I *hate making big decisions! It's so stressful. God, would you just give me a neon sign, please? Moving could be super cool and open up new opportunities, but it could also go badly, and I'll be depressed and miserable, and stuck in the middle of nowhere, eleven hours away from my mom. It's not like I have a lot else tying me here, besides the comfort of my parents and familiarity with the area. I mean, my job is fine, but I don't really see any opportunity for growth or change. And Midland has become such a different city from what I remember as a child. What used to be a safe, small town has turned into a madhouse of big rigs barreling down highways and blocks of temporary housing called "man camps" to accommodate the influx of young men looking to make a quick buck in the oilfield. The oil boom has even made the housing market ridiculous. Since when did the price of a home in Midland come so*

near the price of a similar home in the suburbs of Denver where my sister lived?

My mind swirled with all the pros and cons of moving—lists drawn out on the chalkboard inside my brain. Just a few months before, my sister had her first baby, a girl, the sweetest little angel you can imagine. I longed to be living nearer so that I could be help my sister out and be the cool auntie I'd always wanted to be. But then I would recall the last time I attempted to make my life in Colorado and wound up calling my mom every night in tears due to severe homesickness. I felt like something in me had changed and I would be okay this time, but how could I know for sure?

Just pray about it. That's the answer for everyone facing a big decision. While not wrong, it can feel a bit trite or obtuse when that seems to be the only piece of advice you receive. But the pros-and-cons lists weren't budging and some restlessness inside kept prompting me not to settle, so I prayed. A lot. And then I decided to throw out a little fleece. I started applying for jobs in the Denver area and prayed that if God did not want me to move, I would get zero offers. But if He did want me to move—if He knew the future and that I would survive the distance from my parents—I would get a job offer that week.

This sort of testing God may not always be wise or right. But since I had sincere motives to follow where God wanted me, I believed He would answer my prayer. I filled out a handful of applications to different nursing jobs in the Denver area—mainly working in pediatrics and only willing to take a job with daytime hours as I knew a night shift job would certainly threaten my mental health and recovery. I was in a good place—had been for several years—and was not ready to jeopardize that. It dawned on me that being stable physically and emotionally opens doors to new opportunities. This felt like such a big decision because I really had not been given the opportunity to make these kinds of decisions for myself in the past. I was either too fragile to even consider making a big life move or was on the brink of another full-blown relapse followed by months in residential treatment. This was exciting!

And let me tell you. God answered my prayer! It wasn't exactly a neon sign but close. I received not one but four job offers in a week's time! Anxiety certainly had things to say about the risks of quitting a good stable job where I liked my supervisor and was well-loved by my coworkers to move hundreds of miles away for a job that I hoped I would like but had no assurance or fallback plan. But with Self leading the way, I stuck with my part of the deal to follow through since God had so obviously come through on His part.

※ ※ ※ ※

The move to Colorado proved to be an exciting time of growth and change. Being near my sister and niece (followed by another niece and two nephews) was an enormous blessing and joy. Did I miss my parents? Yes. But I did not cry every night. My new nursing job turned out to be a great fit, and I was able to cross-train to other units, gaining skills in NICU and mom-baby nursing as well as pediatrics.

Another wonderful thing about living near a metroplex is access to care and resources. Since Denver is home to several eating disorder treatment centers and specialists, it is also a hub for outpatient providers in the field. I had soon connected with Bethany, a counselor who specialized in women's issues, trauma, and disordered eating. She introduced me to another powerful therapeutic approach: Eye Movement Desensitization and Reprocessing (EMDR).

EMDR therapy works directly with the nervous system to process traumatic memories. Through bilateral stimulation—typically eye movements or gentle tapping—EMDR helps the brain reprocess trauma that has become stuck in the nervous system. For those of us with eating disorders, trauma often lies at the root of our struggles, whether from childhood experiences, medical trauma, or the eating disorder itself. She also utilized the same IFS therapy modality I was introduced to in residential treatment.

The combination of these therapies proved transformative in decreasing my trauma responses and the dissociation I experienced around early wounds and treatment trauma. Through IFS work I developed a new relationship with my inner world. I grew more adept at noticing when stress would trigger a protector or firefighter part to emerge, attempting to take control through eating disorder behaviors. Instead of automatically following the urge to skip a meal when anxiety rose, I learned to acknowledge these parts with curiosity and compassion. I would recognize the eating disorder part's attempt to help and then gently suggest alternative coping skills, such as crocheting or journaling.

Over time, this internal dialogue became more natural and required less conscious effort. The integration of IFS and EMDR created a foundation for sustainable healing that went beyond mere symptom management to address the deeper wounds driving my eating disorder.

For clinicians reading this, I cannot overemphasize the value of trauma-informed approaches in eating disorder treatment. These modalities offered me tools not just for recovery, but for a fundamental reshaping of my relationship with myself.

An eating disorder–informed dietitian is another key member of a recovery treatment team. In Denver I was blessed to work with an amazing young lady who practices from a weight-neutral approach. With Connie's help, I smashed my scale! That is a big milestone for someone with an eating disorder. Some will argue that if they don't weigh themselves, they won't know if they are slipping backward. But I believe that most people with an eating disorder history, me included, need a substantial amount of time away from the scale before weighing oneself is healthy. An eating disorder is not defined by a number on the scale. Thus, recovery is not defined by a number either. Connie helped me understand how much more important my thoughts and attitudes toward food were as opposed to just measuring progress based on an ability to weigh in at the same number every week for the rest of my life.

Connie was there alongside me during some tumultuous times in my evolving relationship with my body. Becoming comfortable with the changes the body goes through during recovery can be quite challenging.

My thoughts about my body were triggered less by my changing reflection in the mirror and more by changes in sensory input and awareness. For example, when you are used to every piece of clothing, including underwear, fitting loosely, it can be uncomfortable to start experiencing the sensation of material hugging your skin. I was brought back to a distant memory I had as a child of my mother telling me that I would only wear dresses that "didn't touch" me. I wore sack-like dresses with no waistband and baggy jeans and oversized t-shirts. But now I began to piece things together. Even before age eleven when my eating disorder began, I had what would now be labeled as *sensory issues*. Certain fabrics and clothing made me feel uncomfortable or claustrophobic. Bright lights and loud noises caused a feeling of detachment and distress. I can distinctly remember sitting in my room one day looking at my legs in hot pink leggings with white hearts and feeling trapped and itchy inside—they were cutting off my circulation, and my legs felt like lead. But I could not verbalize any of this to my mom.

Through the support of my outpatient team, I was able to understand myself on a deeper level and gain compassion for my unique preferences and needs. In the near future I would find myself turning this compassion outward through professional work as a counselor.

GRAD SCHOOL

Back when I was working as a school nurse, I began to feel God calling me to go back to school for counseling. Many kids at school would come to me complaining of headaches or stomachaches. I would check them over and find no medical reason for their ailments or reason to call their parents to pick them up. On many occasions as they sat in my office where I would agree to allow them some time to just rest before returning to class, they would start to tell me about their mom and dad fighting at home or the anxiety caused by the loud and chaotic lunchroom. Their physical symptoms were real but not caused by influenza or rhinovirus.

While I was hired as the school nurse, I felt that I often acted as a second school counselor. I loved being a listening ear and offering empathy and compassion. But I knew that this was really out of my scope of practice. Sometimes I would imagine how nice it would be to spend a whole hour with these kids, letting them process their emotions. Then one day on my drive home an ad on the Christian radio station I always listened to came on talking about how to apply for a one-thousand-dollar scholarship to Colorado Christian University.

"Make your dream of going back to school a reality. We offer flexible online programs and a Christ-centered education. Graduate degrees in counseling, nursing, teaching, and business available. Just fill out the application form online and you could be on your way to winning one thousand dollars toward your next degree!" The voice cut out and another upbeat song played in its place.

Hmmm, what would it hurt just to apply? I thought. *If I get the scholarship, I'll just take a couple classes in counseling in order to enhance my skills as a nurse and serve my patients better. It's not like I have to get a whole master's degree. That sounds way too long and expensive. And maybe then God will stop nagging at me about the whole going back to school to be a counselor thing. I'm too broken myself to do that but taking a few classes couldn't hurt.*

So, I made a loose promise to God that if I got the scholarship, I would take a thousand dollars' worth of counseling classes. But I continued to let Him know that I could not become a professional counselor because of my own tainted past. *Who would hire someone who has been to rehab five times? No way.*

To make a long story short, I was awarded the scholarship and signed up for two classes in 2018. Several years later that one thousand dollars' worth of classes turned into fifty thousand dollars' worth of classes and a master's degree in clinical mental health counseling. Throughout my journey of healing and recovery, God worked through the wisdom of several trusted mentors to reshape my understanding of what makes an effective counselor. These wise voices helped me recognize that our wounds and struggles, when properly healed and processed, can become wellsprings of empathy and understanding in helping others. The very experiences that once seemed like insurmountable obstacles could be transformed into bridges of connection with those who are still in the midst of their own battles.

In 2021, I took a profound step forward by joining what theologian Henri Nouwen called the "wounded healers," becoming a licensed professional counselor candidate in the state of Colorado. This transition from patient to practitioner represented more than just a career choice; it was a testament to the transformative power of hope and healing.

The magnitude of this achievement becomes even more striking when I reflect on that early psychiatrist's grim prediction. Not only had I survived my twenties— something she had deemed unlikely—but I had gone far beyond mere survival to become a mental health professional myself. God had not just pushed the boundaries of that original prognosis; He had completely rewritten the story. Like a master artist turning what seemed like a ruined canvas into something beautiful and purposeful, He had transformed my struggles into a source of hope and healing for others.

CONCLUSION

So where do we go from here? Further up and further in—to borrow the words of C. S. Lewis.[5] While I have learned and healed immensely, growth and sanctification know no ending in this lifetime. I am not here to tell you that I have arrived or that my life is now just an endless string of triumphs and successes. There are still days when I have to sit Anxiety down and have a little talk. Remind it who is steering the ship and remind my Firefighter parts that their drastic solutions to pea-sized problems will likely result in some rocky fallout on the other side instead of bringing true resolution.

But overall, I have come to a place where my Firefighter and Protector parts—Depression, Anxiety, Eating Disorder, OCD, Perfectionism—do not feel the need to rip the steering wheel out of my hands anymore. My wise inner Self has grown strong and mature. Led by the Holy Spirit I navigate through life's stormy seas using healthy coping strategies and skills. Having my compass fixed on true north—the Word of God and His truth about me instead of the lies of the world—keeps me headed ever *up* and *in*.

CHAPTER TWELVE

CONSIDERATIONS FOR HELPING PROFESSIONALS AND FAMILIES

*W*hen I first entered treatment at eleven years old, I could not have imagined then that the frightened child being admitted to inpatient care would one day become the mental health professional and nurse I am today. Yet here I stand, having traveled both sides of the treatment journey.

My story spans five inpatient and residential stays between childhood and my mid-twenties. Each admission represented both crisis and opportunity—moments when my life hung in a delicate balance between illness and recovery. While these interventions were necessary at points when my life was at risk, I experienced firsthand what research has since confirmed: higher levels of care can come with significant costs beyond the financial.

The research is increasingly clear that intensive treatment settings, while sometimes medically necessary, can create their own challenges. The sense of losing autonomy, being subject to rigid protocols, and experiencing treatment that focuses more on weight restoration than psychological healing can create a trauma of its own. In 2023, the *Journal of Eating Disorders* published a systematic review of real-life experiences of people with anorexia who had undergone inpatient treatment. It brought to light much of what I experienced and have shared in my story. While physiological rehabilitation is essential, the structure and aseptic nature of higher-level treatment facilities for eating disorders can lead to feelings of incarceration, shame, dependence on treatment to maintain recovery, and experiencing depersonalized care.[6]

What I've learned both personally and professionally is that recovery doesn't happen to us; it happens within us. The most effective interventions—whether for eating disorders, depression, or anxiety—honor the person at the center of the experience. Research consistently shows that therapeutic alliance and patient engagement are among the strongest predictors of success in treatment across all mental health conditions.[7]

As clinicians and researchers develop a more sophisticated understanding of eating disorders and co-occurring conditions, the field has begun shifting toward "stepped care" models. These approaches emphasize beginning with the least intensive intervention likely to be effective and scaling up only when necessary. Family-based treatment, specialized outpatient care, partial hospitalization programs, and community-based support have shown remarkable effectiveness when implemented with skill and compassion.

When higher levels of care are necessary—and sometimes they absolutely are—the approach matters profoundly. Treatment environments that maintain dignity, involve patients in decision-making to the extent possible, and focus on developing intrinsic motivation rather than compliance show better long-term outcomes. Programs that avoid punitive measures, provide trauma-informed care, and treat patients as collaborators rather than objects to be fixed help minimize the risk of treatment becoming another trauma to overcome.

My own journey from patient to provider has taught me that healing rarely follows a linear path. Recovery is a complex process of integration—learning to hold the reality of painful experiences while creating space for new possibilities. For professionals working in this field, I offer this perspective: our interventions must be as nuanced and multidimensional as the human beings we serve.

For those currently struggling, I want you to know that your voice matters in your treatment. Research increasingly supports what many of us have known intuitively—that sustainable recovery happens when treatment honors your agency and builds on your strengths rather than focusing exclusively on symptoms. You deserve care that treats you as a whole person, not a diagnosis or a collection of behaviors to be eliminated.

For families navigating these difficult waters, evidence suggests your involvement is crucial. Not as enforcers of treatment protocols, but as supporters of the person you love who is fighting to reclaim their life from illness. The research is clear that family inclusion—implemented skillfully and respectfully—improves outcomes significantly.

For professionals, I urge you to see each patient you encounter as a unique human, created by God, with worth and dignity. Please do not assume that changing pronouns or suppressing hormones is the answer for adolescent girls who are having anxiety about their bodies or saying they wish to be the opposite sex. This is not a political issue. It is an issue of best care for a vulnerable population. The original studies done by the Dutch, by which standards of gender affirming care and early referral for puberty blocking medication relied on, have now been proven unreliable at best.[8] When did the policy of starting with least-invasive treatment go by the wayside? I pray that those who write practice and policy standards will quickly return to reason and lead with treating gender dysphoria—a mental health diagnosis—with psychotherapy as first line.

And if you count yourself among the "helping professionals," whether as a physician, nurse, psychiatrist, counselor, or other specialty, I implore you to follow the ethics of your profession by practicing beneficence, autonomy, and informed consent. Even minors deserve to be a part of the conversation when it comes to their care. While I do not subscribe to the argument that children should be able to make all choices regarding their bodies without parental oversight, I also firmly believe that there are instances when they should be given a choice and certainly to have a voice and right to developmentally appropriate explanation of treatment they will undergo.

After five times in higher levels of care, I fell under the label of *chronic* and *treatment dependent*. Sadly, this leads many sufferers to give up on the possibility of recovery. This has even led to a tragic trend of some seeking physician assisted suicide as a means of ending their struggle (and often being told they are alleviating their family and healthcare system of the "burden" they cause). Once again, if this had been an option during my time of greatest struggle, I am soberly confident that I would have taken it. Now, I am a strong advocate that every human life—from conception to disabled, to dementia, to the grave and everywhere in between—is precious and valuable. As a registered nurse and licensed professional counselor, I see it as my responsibility and honor to treat each person under my care with utmost compassion, empathy, and dignity and to hold out hope for them even if they have lost hope for themselves. God is capable of healing even the most chronic or terminal of conditions if He so chooses.

The field of mental health treatment continues to evolve, and I believe we are moving, however imperfectly, toward approaches that better honor the complexity of human suffering and healing. My hope is that by sharing my story, I contribute in some small way to that evolution—toward care that is both effective and deeply humane.

If my story offers anything, I hope it's this: recovery is possible, even when it seems impossibly distant. The journey from illness to wellness is rarely straightforward, but each step—even the stumbles—can become part of a larger healing narrative. Transformation happens not just when symptoms subside, but when we integrate our experiences into a new understanding of who we are and who we might become. And, for me at least, when we allow God to be the guiding compass for our lives and anchor during the storms.

As I close this memoir, I stand in a place I could never have imagined as that eleven-year-old child—not fully "cured" (I'm skeptical of that concept because mental illness has a biological factor that I don't believe is every fully "cured") but whole in a way that encompasses both my struggles and my strengths. My experience as a patient informs my work as a provider every day, reminding me that behind every diagnosis is a person with dreams, fears, and the capacity for remarkable resilience.

The journey continues.

ENDNOTES

1   "Social and Economic Cost of Eating Disorders in the United States of America," Deloitte Access Economics and the Harvard T.H. Chan School of Public Health and Boston Children's Hospital, June 2020, https://hsph.harvard.edu/wp-content/uploads/2024/10/Social-Economic-Cost-of-Eating-Disorders-in-US.pdf.

2   2 Corinthians 12:7

3   John 9:3 NIV

4   Jay Earley, *Self-Therapy: A Step-by-Step Guide to Creating Wholeness and Healing Your Inner Child Using IFS, a New, Cutting-Edge Psychotherapy.* 1st ed. (Pattern System Books, 2009).

5   C. S. Lewis, The Last Battle (Harper Trophy, 2000), 197.

6   Rankin, R., Conti, J., Ramjan, L. et al. "A systematic review of people's lived experiences of inpatient treatment for anorexia nervosa: living in a 'bubble'."

Journal of Eating Disorders 11, 95 (2023). https://doi.
org/10.1186/s40337-023-00820-0.

7   Dorothy E. Stubbe, "The Therapeutic Alliance: The
     Fundamental Element of Psychotherapy." Focus
     (American Psychiatric Publishing) vol. 16,4 (2018):
     402-403. doi:10.1176/appi.focus.20180022.
     Opland C, Torrico T J. "Psychotherapy and Therapeutic
     Relationship." [Updated 2024 Oct 6]. In: StatPearls
     [Internet]. Treasure Island (FL): StatPearls Publishing;
     2025 Jan. https://www.ncbi.nlm.nih.gov/books/
     NBK608012/.

8   Abbruzzese, E et al. "The Myth of 'Reliable Research' in
     Pediatric Gender Medicine: A critical evaluation of the
     Dutch Studies-and research that has followed." Journal
     of sex & marital therapy vol. 49,6 (2023): 673-699. doi:
     10.1080/0092623X.2022.2150346.

ABOUT THE AUTHOR

*I*n addition to *Learning to Stay* Michelle published *Petunia Can't Think Still* and *Loving Through the Plexiglass* in 2023. Her writing is driven by her passion for mental health awareness and healing for individuals of all ages. Her professional experience encompasses over a decade of work as a registered nurse in diverse settings, as well as her role as a professional counselor. Recently, she has expanded her services to include parent coaching and speaking engagements. She derives pleasure from educating and supporting others based on her personal and professional knowledge. She also is passionate about family, church, and time in nature.

Michelle got married in 2020, in her backyard, in the midst of working full time as a nurse during the COVID-19 pandemic. In 2023 Michelle and her husband adopted their daughter, who has special needs but continues to astound the doctors with her resilience and determination to overcome the odds. Marriage, adoption, and motherhood have brought many new adventures and challenges that we can only hope will be shared in a future publication.

www.ingramcontent.com/pod-product-compliance
Lightning Source LLC
Chambersburg PA
CBHW031528120626
46545CB00005B/2048